AF067449

Islam

Islam

Between Divine Message and History

by
Abdelmajid Sharfi

CEU PRESS
Central European University Press
Budapest • New York

© 2000 by Abdelmajid Sharfi

English translation © 2005 by Huda Fakhreddine

First published in Arabic as *Al-Islam bayn ar-risālah wa't-tārīkh* in 2000 by *Dar at-Talīʿa*, Beirut

English edition published in 2005 by

Central European University Press

An imprint of the
Central European University Share Company
Nádor utca 11, H-1051 Budapest, Hungary
Tel: +36-1-327-3138 or 327-3000
Fax: +36-1-327-3183
E-mail: ceupress@ceu.hu
Website: www.ceupress.com

400 West 59th Street, New York NY 10019, USA
Tel: +1-212-547-6932
Fax: +1-212-548-4607
E-mail: mgreenwald@sorosny.org

All rights reserved. No part of this publication may be reproduced, stored in a retrieval system, or transmitted, in any form or by any means, without the permission of the Publisher.

ISBN 963 9241 87 3 cloth
ISBN 963 7326 16 2 paperback

Sharfi, Abdelmajid.
[Al-Islam bayn ar-risala wa't-tarikh. English]
Islam between divine message and history / by Abdelmajid Sharfi.
p. cm.
Includes index.
ISBN 9639241873 (hardbound) -- ISBN 9637326162 (pbk.)
1. Islam--History. 2. Islam--Essence, genius, nature. I. Title.

BP50.S47 2005
297.2--dc22

2005002933

Printed in Hungary by

CONTENTS

Introduction 1

PART ONE

Chapter One - The Theoretical and Historical Background 13

Chapter Two – The Mohammedan Mission 27

Chapter Three - The Characteristics of the Mohammedan Mission 45

Chapter Four - The Issue of Legislation (Tashri[c]) 58

Chapter Five - The Seal of Prophecy 86

PART TWO

Introduction to Part Two 99

Chapter Six - The Prophet's Caliphate 101

Chapter Seven - Institutionalizing Religion 117

Chapter Eight - Theorizing for the Institution 131

Epilogue 192

Index 199

INTRODUCTION

What is the purpose of this book? What can it add to the many writings that have already probed Islam as a history, a doctrine, a law, and a code of ethics? I believe that the bulk of Islamic thought today is either a repetition and regurgitation—often distorted by oversimplifications—of what the ancients have said, or an adaptation and projection in which ideology replaces real knowledge, or a discussion of partial issues which lacks a comprehensive view and a clear theoretical framework. What Islamic thought produces today is at best a voicing of intentions and a proclamation of desiderata. It constantly refers to the difficulty of achieving its own declared aims and, rather than making any explicit statements, resorts to allusions in an attempt to dissimulate and to play safe.

There are two main reasons for this failure to present a vision that combines loyalty to Islam, as a mission valid for all times and places, with the imperatives of modern consciousness. The first, and more important, is the cultural backwardness of contemporary Islamic societies, which do not actively interact with what advanced societies produce in the fields of science and learning, technology, innovation, values, and sentiments. They are traditional and conservative in their ways, and their relations with the West, the source and origin of present-day civilization, are embattled as a result of western colonialism in the recent past and of western hegemony in all its different forms. That is why these societies, in their relations with the West, fluctuate between antagonism and infatuation. They are still seeking to balance their conflicting needs. In the light of all this, it is only natural that, with the exception of the elite and the educated, they have no great urge to review and reconsider their heritage and are not prepared to accept anything that is not familiar and established by habit and custom.

The second reason is that religious studies have often been the exclusive domain of people with a traditional education. These, as a result of their intellectual make-up, are incapable of keeping in step with developments in the field of modern knowledge that have a bearing on the phenomenon of religion as a whole. They remain captives of an old, out-dated vision which can only faintly relate to the developing present. Conversely, people with a modern education are not overly interested in religious matters. They either live in complete isolation from the reality of their societies or they suffer from a deep division between their practical and intellectual lives on one hand and their spiritual lives on the other. Moreover, they are generally forbidden to express themselves and declare their opinions freely. This oppression practiced by the state or social pressure goes hand in hand with fear and suspicion of all that is not familiar and established by habit and custom.

However, Islamic societies are not homogeneous either collectively or individually. Some are still dominated by traditional modes of life and production, while others have progressed in varying degrees on the road to modernization, whether at the level of institutions, at the level of industrialization and the adoption of modern means of production and services, or especially at the level of social relationships, including the family and the progress that has taken place with regard to the status of women and to the content and expansion of education.

Based on these facts, this book bets on the future. It tries as much as possible to respond to the needs of those who are rapidly becoming integrated in modern life, and to the aspiration of the rising generations to an Islamic thought that is capable of taking account of the four major revolutions witnessed by humanity since the end of the Middle Ages in Europe. The first revolution was Copernicus's discovery that the earth is not the center of the universe, as the ancients believed, but only a small planet in the solar system, a fact investigated and proven by modern astronomy. The second revolution was the establishment of the theory of evolution since Darwin and man's loss of that special status which was thought to distinguish him from the rest of the animals. Freud and the school of psychoanalysis represented a third revolution by inferring that man's behavior is not fully controlled by the conscious will but is in fact subject to the influence of the unconscious, the repressed, and the hidden drives. The fourth revolution is what the world is witnessing now in the rapid progress of biotechnology and genetic engineering, with the resulting power to control life and to alter the natural qualities of plants, animals, and even humans, which were once thought to be stable and fixed.

If we add to these major revolutions in knowledge all the other changes that have occurred—the transformation of our way of life through the development of industry and the practical application of science in general (including the affordability and advancement of transportation, the availability of information, and countless other amenities); the modification of our social structures, value systems, and daily practices, which have resulted from these developments; our knowledge of the most delicate and most general laws which govern human civilization, the basis of doctrines and rituals, human psychology, and the determinants of behavior and thought, which anthropology and sociology have provided over the past two centuries—then my work needs no further justification. Those who want to think for themselves and not through others will realize that what I aspire to here is to attain an end for which I have made the greatest efforts and benefited from tens of studies which have helped to illuminate some of the dark untrodden paths I have ventured upon.

The Muslim reader has grown accustomed to hearing the call for free reasoning (*'ijtihād*) as a necessity both decreed by religion and dictated by the age we live in. Through this modest endeavor, I wish to participate in substantiating this call for reasoning. However, it is necessary first to clear up a serious ambiguity which might lead to misunderstandings and useless arguments. In the old days ordinary people emulated *al-Mujtahid* (the applier of personal reasoning), whereas today the opinions expressed by the *Mujtahid* places an obligation on him alone. The *'ijtihād* required today is not the peremptory or absolute *'ijtihād* in the fundamental juridical sense, which is used to deduce juridical judgements in cases that cannot be referred to any texts, and which is part of a system that in my view can be overcome. Furthermore, I maintain that such *'ijtihād* is useless if not impossible, unless we consider the "tropes" which some people unconsciously resort to in order to bestow an Islamic coloring on what is non-Islamic. The *'ijtihād* that is required must therefore be a kind of speculation and meditation that remains loyal to the essence of the Mohammedan Mission but that dares, where necessary, to challenge any postulates established on the presumption that they are "known of religion by necessity." It must be an *'ijtihād* which cannot be rejected on the basis of what so-and-so has said, since "it considers what was said rather than who said it," and since it defends the rights of the successors rather than sanctifying the predecessors. I believe that the time has come to set in motion a debate concerning the core of the issues in question, a debate that would target the essence and the center, avoiding the crusts and the shells.

This work consists of two parts. In the first I have tried to introduce the characteristics of the Mohammedan Mission from a perspective which endeavored to be faithful to its essential purposes and to the historical truth at one and the same time. The second illustrates the different ways in which people have understood the Mission and the reasons which have led them to adopt one specific interpretation of it from the many that were theoretically available. In addition, I present some alternative interpretations which actually existed but did not enjoy any acceptance and popularity on a large scale.

I have deliberately written the original of this book in Arabic although many friends have advised me to write it in a foreign language, in which it would have a better chance of reaching a large number of Muslim readers who do not know any Arabic, particularly in Asia, but also in Europe and America. However, I have preferred in the first instance to address monolingual readers, considering that any Arab reader who is conversant with a foreign language is in any case likely to acquire wider horizons, to think for himself, and to abandon repetition and duplication. Such a reader in more than one language needs a work of this kind less than one who has only a traditional education and who cannot even imagine the benefits of modern knowledge with its admirable discoveries and methods as well as its problems and unresolved issues.

Moreover, it is the duty of the speakers of Arabic to subject their language to the thinking methods of this age to ensure that it does not ossify and turn into a dead weight. That is why I aspire to participate, from my own modest position, in a process that I regard as inevitable. It is the process of "internalizing" modern concepts and at the same time avoiding the pitfalls of a false scientism where science becomes a synonym for mystification and where the use of a high-sounding jargon becomes a means to hide confused and unclear ideas. Without doubt, the balance is hard to maintain. For one feels that words betray one, especially when one attempts to express a new concept without resorting to outlandish terms or terms with unintended or unwelcome connotations.

Since this book is not an academic study in the narrow sense, my references are not necessary for an understanding of its contents. My footnotes are intended to direct readers to material for verification or further study. I hope that the opinions and views presented here will serve as a starting point for more profound and productive research that would complement and rectify my own work where necessary.

The interest of modern western studies in religion did not begin in a clerical context, but in the context of philosophy on one hand and sociology on the other. This interest concurred with the prevailing positivist and scientific tendencies. Thus, the theories of Feuerbach, Marx, Comte, Frazer, Durkheim, and others, despite the differences in their inclinations and orientations, were influenced by these tendencies to such an extent that they considered religion only as one of the many stages of human development towards pure rationality. Furthermore, they considered religion as a projection of human desires, as a surrogate for needs unfulfilled in reality, and even as a pathological phenomenon. At best, and as a result of Eurocentrism, Christianity was considered as the most highly developed religion and thus as uniquely worthy of survival.

Today these theories have only historical value. The history of religions, or rather the general study of religion, has gradually become independent of anthropology and sociology. Since the beginning of the twentieth century, and thanks to the work of outstanding scholars such as the Italian Pettazzoni, the Romanian Eliade, and the Frenchmen Dumezil and Le Bras, it has acquired its own fields of research and its own methods, which are primarily based on the comparison of elements that are suitable for comparison and on an understanding of religion as a specific phenomenon that cannot be allocated to anthropology or any other branch of knowledge. The study of religion has greatly benefited from new research in sociology, anthropology, linguistics, and history. It has also benefited from the methods of phenomenology, semantics, psychological analysis, the study of myth and fantasy, and many other approaches which have led scholars away from scientism and from the habit of assigning to rationality a unique status within the broad spectrum of human concerns.

As a result of this development, the struggle between reason and religion or between knowledge and faith–inherited from the past and in particular from the nineteenth century–has receded into the background, as the phenomenon of religion was acknowledged to have a uniqueness, authenticity and power of its own. However, this acknowledgement was not a blank check. It forced religious people to shed many illusions and accretions that had been attached to religion in the course of history, making it perform certain social roles which were not necessarily germane to it and exploiting it for purposes for which there was no longer the same need as before in modern social systems.

It is from this perspective that I will try to apply the results and methods of modern research to Islam, bearing in mind that it shares with other religions–mainly Christianity and Judaism–the characteristic of submission to laws and rules, and that at the same time it has some unique characteristics which prevent its assimilation into any other religion.

My intention to apply modern methods is due to the fact that Islam is not a dead religion, which is studied like an object in a museum. It is a living religion, which was understood and practiced by successive generations of the ancients according to their knowledge and their historical circumstances. Moreover, Muslims in our own day still strongly feel that its message concerns them. They look to it for answers to their own questions and not to the questions of their fathers or grandfathers. They hope that it will offer adequate solutions, which would constitute, without undue pressure, the basis of their belief and commitment.

It is important to note that the reading I suggest here is one that tries to move away from the substantivist views of Islam. Many books and articles by distinguished Muslims or non-Muslims contain assertions such as: Islam rejects the separation between the spiritual and the temporal; Islam calls for reason; Islam carries the seeds of hostility towards its adversaries; Islam honors women; Islam degrades women. In fact, Islam is exempt from all such judgements presented as final and established facts beyond any argument. Despite the specific features, which bind its followers and distinguish them from the followers of other religions or from non-believers, there is not one Islam, and there never has been, either in time or in space.

Islam has been able to adapt to many different and conflicting circumstances. It has adapted to hereditary monarchies and electoral republics, to Socialism and Capitalism, to innovation and convention, to contraception and the lack of it, to nomadism and to civilization. No one can claim that his or her Islam is the true Islam. Islam is a call to all humans to achieve and fulfill their humanity as best they can. Each responds to this call in accordance with his or her personal and general circumstances, education, disposition, mental horizons, and financial and moral capabilities. What matters is the extent to which the exegesis (*Ta'wīl*), accepted by Muslims of all groups and all generations, responds to the needs of the present time, whether these needs be social or intellectual. For whenever there is harmony between a Muslim's consciousness and his actual being, religion has performed a positive function. Whenever they are separate and out of harmony, religion is merely an expression of nostalgia and hope. In the latter case it is a compensation for impotence and defeat, or an external bond between members of a nation, which is soon severed when other bonds, such as nationality or other ideologies that can perform the same binding function, come into being.

The significance of this method lies in the fact that it will lead believers to reconsider their own axioms, or what they had thought to be the postulates of religion. This will make it possible to overcome the exclusionist views that have long wrecked the relationships between people because of differences in their beliefs or their religious traditions, even if they were advocates of dialogue and tolerance, and even if they respected the opinions of others and their right to express themselves freely.

Any stand based on adherence to a specific understanding regarded as the sole truth, to a certain ritual of worship thought indispensable, or to some specific religious form of behavior believed to be decisive between right and wrong, can only lead–intentionally or unintentionally–to the elimination of the other. It also bestows a sense of finality on what is relative by its very nature because it is interpreted by humans or linked to historical circumstances, which in their turn are subject to human interpretation.

I would like to thank all those who made this work possible and in particular those responsible for the *Wissenschaftskolleg zu Berlin*, with all its employees and librarians. My stay there gave me a chance to devote a whole year to research in ideal conditions for reading, writing and engaging in stimulating and rewarding debates.

PART ONE

CHAPTER ONE

THE THEORETICAL AND HISTORICAL BACKGROUND

The prophetic mission in a general sense can relatively easily be defined as a message that the prophet-messenger took upon himself to convey to his contemporaries and, through them, to a specific nation and to all humanity. However, the exegeses of this mission and its content remain infinitely diverse. Determining the meaning of *nubuwwa* (prophethood) or *waḥi* (revelation) is one of the most difficult tasks that may confront a scholar. It is a variable concept, which changes with different religions, cultures, and times. Moreover, it relates to God, "that mystery which separates us when revealed and which unites us when it remains abiding within."[1] Grasping the concept of *nubuwwa* or *waḥi* and pinning it down to a definition is made even more difficult by the fact that it refers to unique historical experiences, which are impossible to recapture. Those who had these experiences were certainly human, but they were nonetheless endowed with traits not found in ordinary people. Thus

[1] Meslin, M., "Introduction" to Pettazione, R., *Religione e Società*, Bologna, 1996, p. 15. Al-Karmānī states that God is not material and thus cannot be perceived by the senses, and nor can He be perceived by reason. Moreover, no language can contain Him or express the concept of Him. Thus, man is by nature incapable of a complete understanding of God, and God by His essence resists perception. See Rāḥat al-Aql (The Comfort of the Mind), Cairo, 1953. Victor Hugo's little known posthumous book *Dieu* (God), Paris, 1969, 3 vols., also contains some most enjoyable reading on the subject.

they attracted many adherents, disciples, and votaries, who believed their teaching and struggled to disseminate it. The belief of these followers was spontaneous and needed no prompting. It involved no theorizing or speculation, which was a later process that only began after the time of the missions. In the early history of Islamic thought, theories did not constitute a major concern or research topic, for they only occurred in the sphere of theology, which in turn was initially related to political issues rather than being a systematic rationalization of the content of faith.

Therefore, before questioning the Qur'ānic text, I must step back for a while from the arguments of scholastic theologians and consider what the history of religions tells us about *nubuwwa* and *waḥi*. This questioning of the text will attempt to penetrate the thick layers of exegesis, which obscure and mislead as much as they reveal and enlighten, and will aim to approach the historical truth as closely as possible. Nor can I avoid turning to the accounts of the *sīra* (the prophet's biography) although I know that they were recorded after the events they relate. I am also aware that these accounts were influenced by the circumstances of their compilers (Ibn Saᶜd, Ibn Isḥāq Ibn Hishām, al-Tabari) and by all the events in the lives of the Muslims after the prophet's death, particularly in the transitional period between the time of the prophet and the time of recording. In other words, the *sīra* is a specific representation of the events of the prophet's life with all the ambiguities to which any representation is subject and which must be treated with caution. It is quite evident that the collective memory, rather than preserving the real components of a hero's life, turns him into an "archetype" that embodies all the traits necessary for the role assigned to him. Nor are these traits merely cited but they are displayed in a manner indicative of the characteristics this model figure is meant to represent.

Throughout history, the manifestations of the sacred and the forms of religiousness have undergone a myriad of variations, which are manifested by excavations and archeological discoveries, the beliefs of "primitive" peoples, the so-called mystic religions, and, of course, the prophetic *waḥi* or revelation.

In this context I do not intend to go into any detail about the characteristics of ancient beliefs or doctrines, such as the annual ritual festivities held in most agricultural societies at the beginning and end of the fertile season. These rituals were related to death, birth, puberty, marriage, illness, and other crucial events in life. They also included the consecration of trees and places as well as some natural phenomena such as the sun, the moon, and other planets, the adoption of idols and the deification of kings, legends of kings and deities, etc. Their diversity, profusion, and complexity makes them extremely difficult to summarize without distortion. What concerns me most in this history are the characteristics of the main phases that man passed through in his search for the meaning of existence on this earth, as he strove to comprehend his origin and his fate, and to invent an order of things in an attempt to escape from the chaos that appears to engulf all creatures.

Man can only live in a systemized world, no matter what the system may be. Thus, it is inevitable that he should attempt to harmonize in his mind both the human social phenomena and the natural ones, and to seek justifications to protect these phenomena from the charge of arbitrariness. In the process of producing the constituents of that system, man in fact creates what differentiates him from animals: he creates culture. Culture in this sense includes moral as well as material achievements. However, as time passes, the new devices, institutions, and values become more and more independent of their source, and seem to acquire their own logic. As a result, man adopts and retains them as if they were postulates inherent in the "nature of things." In other words, he "internalizes" them, as the social epistemologists put it, and submits to them with absolute spontaneity, forgetting that it was he who produced them in the first place.[2] And so it continues. Past human achievements become the foundation of new ones, which in their turn acquire an objective tinge and an existence of their own, as man "internalizes" them and their seeming objectivity in a continuous dialectic and interplay. That is why in ancient times man lived in a mystery, unconscious of the significance of his deeds and behavior at both the individual and the collective level.

For example, man lays down rules and restrictions governing sexual relationships. Such restrictions, despite numerous differences between them, exist in all cultures. They define what is permissible and licit, and what is forbidden and illicit. Eventually, they become constituents of man's own personality. In fact man defines himself through the eyes of others. If his social upbringing is completely successful, the set rules acquire a certain spontaneity and intuitiveness, preventing the individual violating them. What is more, he cannot even imagine himself violating them without feeling guilt and remorse. And if he happens to disregard these rules and is punished for doing so, he considers himself, in his own mind, as guilty and deserving of that punishment. The same applies to all other social relationships. Complete commitment to the rules and restrictions prevalent in a group leads man to accept reality as it is, without ever entertaining the thought of objecting to it or violating it. Indeed, he can see no other alternative to what the group has established and agreed upon. This may even lead him to sacrifice himself willingly for these rules, as in a war or feud in which the tribe, the populace, or the nation participates.

[2] See P. Berger, *The Social Reality of Religion*, Penguin Books, 1973. Part I, pp. 13-107. This book was first published in 1967 under the title *The Sacred Canopy*. In 1971 it was translated into French and published by Centurion under the title *La religion dans la conscience moderne* (Religion in Modern Consciousness). I translated it into Arabic with a group of friends and it was published in 2003 by CPU (Tunis).

Historically, religion has played a major role in this process of justification and legitimization of various social experiments by investing social institutions with an authority that goes beyond their experimental nature and that presents them within a frame of reference in which they acquire both holiness and universality. From that perspective, these institutions are seen as a reflection and manifestation of the structure of the universe itself. The constant circular movement of the universe is manifested in the succession of natural phenomena. Through this circular movement the universe continually emerges from chaos, and man symbolically recreates that emergence in his behavior in relation to changes in the weather. This feature, alongside other features of a doctrinal coloring, is what really characterizes the most ancient forms of religion, where the essentially fragile phenomena of human activity acquire a touch of stability and constancy. Moreover, some characteristics which are usually attributed to the gods are attributed to these phenomena, allowing them to overcome the death of individuals and groups by being embedded in a sacred time.

Although it has accompanied all religions, the process of justification and legitimization in primitive religions initially occurred in the context of revival and of a vision of the universe which did not separate man from nature. That is why these religions, in addition to adopting a number of fundamental myths which explain existence in general, acquired an obvious magical touch, where words uttered by a certain qualified individual could influence the course of events, and where collective rituals obtained a major role in preserving the balance of life and integrating the individual into the group.[3]

[3] On the issue of ancient belief cf. the studies of Mircea Eliade, in particular *Le sacré et la profane* (The Sacred and the Profane), Paris, 1965, *La nostalgie des origines* (Nostalgia for Origins), Paris, 1971 and *Histoire des croyances et des idées religieuses* (The History of Beliefs and Religious Ideas), 3 vols, Paris, 1976–1983, as well as many other works cited in these two studies.

The widespread phenomenon of offering sacrifices to supernatural forces in cosmological religions belongs in this context. The immolation of a human being—a first-born son or a virgin—in some cases, or of a certain animal in most, aimed not only at propitiating the gods or bringing about fertility, but primarily at re-establishing a lost balance. Sacrifices were regarded as necessary in the event of droughts, floods, violent winds, earthquakes and other natural disasters, and likewise when customs and social laws were violated. Those who practiced rituals, including the offering of sacrifices, were aware of the magical-religious quality of their acts, and hoped that such behavior would maintain the familiar forms of life. The stock of domestic animals, the supply of game animals, the fruit on the trees, the crops in the fields, the birth of children without deformities, the succession of the seasons and of day and night, the regularity of the natural phenomena in general, all depended on the practice of rituals. If the system was disrupted for some reason or other, man considered himself responsible for that disruption and regarded it as his duty to perform the appropriate rituals in order to re-establish things as they were.

This type of religious feeling continued in various forms throughout the periods that preceded history in its usual sense, particularly before man learned to write and before the complex systems of advanced historical religions emerged. It is not my intention in this context to touch upon the Indian or Asiatic systems in general, for their influence on the monotheistic religions that emerged in the Middle East was quite limited. But it is definitely worth noting that traces of doctrines rooted in antiquity remain present in the monotheistic systems and that their effects are still obvious in the Holy Bible of the Christians and the Jews. Examples of such traces are the acknowledgement of the "magical" or thaumaturgic effect of words uttered in certain special contexts, the preservation of one of the ancient ontological features manifested in the view that plants and animals have no real existence until they are given names, or the idea, common in Sumeric beliefs, that man was created from clay. Among the many elements surviving in the Old Testament's Story of Genesis, the characteristics of Paradise as portrayed there contain visions of Mesopotamia as well as some obvious Babylonian features. Adam eating from the tree of knowledge, which symbolizes man's failure to attain immortality, recalls Gilgamesh's failure to attain the same goal. The Guidance (*hadi*) spoken of in the Torah, although it accompanied various forms of religion rooted in antiquity and practiced in various ways by most peoples, belongs to the Canaanite system of endearment or requesting favors where the sacrifices offered were considered as food for the gods. Moreover, the stone monuments which symbolized the divine presence were known to the Arabs of the Peninsula before the Torah. Offerings and sacrifices were presented to these stones, especially at the beginning of spring, in addition to many other religious symbols and rituals which were known in the region and subsequently retained, with new connotations, in the Torah.

Although the new element in Judaism was the belief in one god, the Torah does not deny the existence of many gods as much as it emphasizes that Moses has only one God, who insists on being one God alone. Initially the god of the Canaanites was Baal, until the Jews confused him with Eil and Yahweh. Eventually, all three became one god. They were not kept apart, and the belief in Baal was not rejected until the seventh or eighth century B.C. Moreover, Yahweh, as portrayed in the Torah, resembles man; he loves and hates, forgives and vindicates, etc., but he does not have the faults of the Greek gods, and in particular he refuses to be mocked.

Nevertheless, the presence of ancient beliefs in the monotheistic systems must not obscure the novelty of these systems and the break they represented with what went before. Even Yahweh's likeness to man is nothing but one of his two forms of manifestation. The other form is the one that does not reflect the human condition: it is the "other" in the full sense of the word, solitary, without family, wife or children, but surrounded by all divine beings. Yahweh is similar to an absolute ruler. He seems to symbolize the desire for complete perfection and ultimate purity. Thus it is not surprising that we find in monotheism traces of the struggle between metaphysical forces that was familiar to many other religions, nor that the champions of monotheism throughout the ages have had a fanatical desire to emulate the divine traits. Furthermore, Yahweh, unlike the Hindu gods, attributes great value and importance to ethics and practical morality. That is why certain historical events have, in the course of time, gained a religious significance as divine manifestations. Another novelty was the prohibition on eating from the tree, which revealed a new idea unrelated to the symbolic meaning for which it had stood before. This new idea concerned the value of existential knowledge and the fact that knowledge can radically change the structure of human existence.[4]

However, the true novelty and most important contribution of monotheism was that of making man responsible for his own deeds, especially the bad ones, and the absolution granted by God. In the Torah, God addresses man for the first time when he addresses Abraham. He demands some things from him and promises him others, but He is not affected by man's subsequent behavior and He is in no way in need of man. Man's disobedience no longer disrupts the balance of the universe as it did before, and the relationship that now binds him to God is that of Faith. Those who used to offer sacrifices were aware of their religious value, whereas Abraham does not understand the importance of his being asked to sacrifice his son. When he sets out to kill Isaac, he is merely responding to the call of faith, and this faith is what helps him—man in general—to endure the hard-

[4] *Pace* the objection of Durand, who believes that eating from the tree is symbolic of death and not of knowledge. See Durand, G., *Les structures anthropologiques de l'imaginaire* (The Anthropological Structures of the Imaginary), Paris, 1973, p. 125.

ships and trials of life. Both Job and Abraham represent a perfect model of that deep faith, which is unshakable despite the difficult choices man faces.

Historians of religion generally reject the idea of a linear development from polytheism to monotheism, and insist on the unity of the human soul. However, this is not to deny that monotheism represented, in many respects, a major and characteristic shift in religious history. It reduced the magical dimension, establishing a historical view of events, and setting up a rational legislative system. The concept of prophethood also developed. Prophecy, as a state of mental intoxication, was familiar to the Canaanite religion around 1000 B.C. The prophets the Jews encountered in Palestine co-existed with the "foreseers" of their Bedouin period. But later on, the concept of the prophet and that of the "seer" merged into one.

There were two types of prophets: those who dwelt near places of worship and performed rituals together with monks (and who were accused of lying), and those who conveyed their message not as members of the foreseeing profession, attached to the temples, but as chosen messengers of God. They had the ability to know the unseen and to defy the laws of nature. When they were prophesying or receiving auguries, they were overcome by paralysis, fainting, convulsions and other unusual states. They were especially aware of the fact that they were not speaking of their own accord but, rather, conveying the word of God and transmitting His commands and prohibitions. Those individuals who appeared in particular between the eighth and the fifth century B.C. are the ones whose prophecies were recorded and preserved in the Old Testament. They include Ezekiel, Amos, Jeremiah, and others, whereas Abraham, Lot, Isaac, and Jacob (Israel) were described as the Fathers and not as prophets. However, what is noteworthy here is that prophethood, in the sense of conveying a message from God, was a Jewish phenomenon, and this explains the objections to the prophethood of Mohammed when he appeared among the *Ummiyūn*.[5] The *Ummiyūn*, here, are the "Gentiles," i.e. the non-Jews, and not those who cannot read or write, as many believe.[6]

When Jesus appeared in Palestine, all his contemporaries—those who believed in him as well as those who did not—could only view him through the perspective of prophethood available in Jewish circles, that is, as the Messiah, or the savior of his people from the yoke of the foreign occupier, and as the sign of the approaching end of the world and the dawn of a new era in which the lamb would peacefully graze next to the wolf. As for his paradoxical relationship with God, the idea of the incarnation in him of the divine, the connection between that incarnation and the word (Logos), and the concept of redemption were all created by the first generation of Christians after the separation of the church from Judaism—in particular under the influence of Paul—and after the spread of the new religion among the "gentiles" in those regions under the sway of Hellenism, Greek philosophy and various Gnostic doctrines.[7]

The Arab Peninsula in general, particularly Ḥijāz, was by no means isolated from the religions and cultural currents that existed in the Middle East, whether in Syria or Palestine, Egypt or Mesopotamia, or neighboring Persia. The concept of political borders, separating and isolating regions from each other, did not exist at that time. Thus there were con-

[5] The word *Ummiyūn* in Arabic means those who cannot read or write, but it can also mean gentiles, i.e. non-Jews. [Translator's note]

[6] See Ahmad Shaḥlan, "Mafhūm al ummiyya fi al-Qur'ān" (The Concept of the Gentile in the Qur'ān) in *Majallat Kulliyyat al Ādāb wa al-ᶜulūm al insān-niyya*, Revue de la Faculté des Lettres et Sciences Humaines, Université Mohamed V, Rabat, Issue 1 (1977), p. 103–125. The writer concludes from his analysis that the gentiles are people without a book and without a religion. They still behave according to their natural instincts and they do not have a holy book.

[7] See the first part of the thesis Abdelmajid Sharfi, *al Fikr al Islāmī fi ar-Rad ᶜalā an-Nasārā* (Muslim Thought in Response to Christianity), Tunis/ Algiers, 1986.

stant exchanges, of both a trading and a non-trading kind, between the peoples of these regions, even in times of war and famines, together with the mutual influences that accompany such exchanges. The *ḥajj*, or pilgrimage to Mecca, on one hand, and the markets, on the other, provided opportunities for the mingling and interaction of doctrines and ideas. Thus we must regard the rise of Islam at the beginning of the seventh century not only as a natural extension of the monotheistic religions in the Jewish and Christian regions, but also as a continuation of the phenomenon of religion in general throughout human history. In doing so, we must not neglect the environmental and circumstantial factors related to Mecca and its surroundings, but neither must we accept that the features of the new message were solely determined by reactions against, or the adoption of, elements of the Arabic pre-Islamic tradition, as it is usually claimed in modern western studies of the rise of Islam, which are still influenced by what was purported about it in medieval Europe.[8] Therefore, the Mohammedan mission presents itself as a continuation of past missions, but supported by a firm historical method.

Monotheism first appeared with Judaism, but was marked by reification and bore many traces of past doctrines.[9] For example, God was sometimes addressed in the plural form as "Elohim," which stood for a national god of a specially

[8] An example of such studies is J. Chabbi, *Le Seigneur des tribus. L'Islam de Mohamet*, Paris: Noesis, 1997. This book is based on extensive knowledge and it attempts to employ a philological method, but its perspective remains limited and it lacks the comprehensive historical vision that could acknowledge the naturally outstanding position of Islam in the monotheistic system.

[9] The following three books by Lods are considered classical works on this subject: *Israel des origines au VIIIe siècle avant notre ère*, Paris, 1930; *Les prophètes d'Israel et les debuts du Judaisme*, Paris, 1935; *La religion d'Israel*, Paris, 1939. See also Max Weber, *Antikes Judentum* (Ancient Judaism, translated into French as *Le Judaisme antique*, Paris, 1970).

designated people, and not a universal god. Moreover, rituals and various prohibitions occupied an important place in the Old Testament, in addition to the fact that early Judaism did not accept the idea of resurrection or life after death.[10] Subsequently, the Christian belief in the doctrines of the Trinity and the Incarnation, the unique status of Mary, and the beneficial powers of saints and their remains led to various deviations from pure monotheism. It has been established that the religious achievements of the Jewish and Christian groups inhabiting Ḥijāz and the north and south of the Arab Peninsula were neither high nor refined. For none of these groups, with the exception of the Christians of Ḥīra, is known for any significant contribution to the theoretical and theological output, for example, of Syria and Egypt. In the interaction between the culture of the adherents of these two monotheistic religions and local folk traditions, Bedouin lore with its oral features prevailed. This resulted in a deviation from the official doctrine held by the highly intellectual bishops and theologians, who had direct access to the sources of the doctrine.

At the beginning of the seventh century, Ḥijāz had the potential to accept the new religion. The impact of the tribal communities had begun to weaken as a result of Mecca's rise to a position of power, influence and control as a center of religious and economic life in the whole of the Arab Peninsula. The wars between the Empires of Persia and Byzantium and the resulting weakness of Yemen played an essential role in diverting the international trade routes between Asia, Europe, and Africa. This allowed the traders of the Quraysh tribes to appropriate these routes, particularly since they had already succeeded, as a result of īlāf (unification), in securing the caravans loaded with goods and in giving the tribes

[10] On this subject see the collective work *Histoire des religions en Europe, Judaisme, Christianisme, et Islam* (The History of Religions in Europe: Judaism, Christianity, and Islam), Paris, Hachette, 1999, p. 35.

whose regions of influence the caravans crossed a share in the profits of this trade.[11] The fortune gained from trade, together with the symbolic gains resulting from the pilgrimage to Mecca and the monopoly in the care of the pilgrims led to an implicit acknowledgement of the superiority of the Quraysh. A further cause of this acknowledged superiority was the contribution of the Quarysh to the organization of life in Mecca and to the establishment of an institutional nucleus made up of the wealthy of every tribe, who met in council (*dār an-nadwa*) to discuss a variety of matters that concerned the group and to determine the behavior that the individual members were expected to observe.

These changes, which occurred from the sixth century A.D. in the order of the Arab Peninsula in general and in Ḥijāz in particular, were to have a great influence on the standards of religious life. For, in parallel with the levelling of accents and the emergence of a common literary language evident in the collection of seven major poems, called the *Mu'allaqāt* and in the production of the sixth-century poets in general, the ascendancy of the Quraysh facilitated a convergence of doctrines and rituals. It also enabled a number of individuals to seek new religious modes that were better suited to the new condition despite its defects and shortcomings, and to aspire further to the spiritual nourishment lacking in the pagan doctrines connected with the traditional tribal system which had begun to show symptoms of dissolution.[12] Thus, some of the Arabs of the Peninsula embraced Christianity, the only evangelizing religion available, since Judaism, which was exclusive to the Israelites, was not open to newcomers. Others preferred to steer away from the wor-

[11] See Victor Sahab, *Ilaf Quraysh (*The Unification of the Quraysh*)*, Beirut, 1992.

[12] "Le respect des traditions est, dans son principe même, un facteur de dissolution des structures" (The respect for tradition is, as a matter of principle, a factor for the dissolution of structures), J. Duvignaud, *Chebika*, Tunis, 1994, p. 115.

ship of idols and to believe in one god, the god of Abraham and of his son Ishmael, the grandfather of the Arabs: they were known as the Hanafites (*al aḥnāf*). In other words, the period in which Islam emerged was a period of change at all levels; a time that called for individuals who could bring great hopes and open up wide horizons. And it was Mohammed, the son of ᶜAbdullah, who carried out this mission.

CHAPTER TWO

THE MOHAMMEDAN MISSION

If we were to compare what we know of Mohammed with what we know of other great men—such as Confucius, Buddha, Zoroaster, Moses, and Jesus—who had a profound and lasting influence on history, we find that Mohammed, unlike them, was always in the spotlight. Nevertheless, even the earliest and most reliable reports on his life that have reached us are tinged by the mythical mentality that dominated the thought of the ancients. The Muslims' aspiration to emulate their prophet's personality and way of life was influenced by pre-Islamic and non-Islamic role models. This led to a deviation from reality and, in many cases, to a mythologizing of that personality.[13] The only counterweight to this tendency was the image of Mohammed presented by the Qur'ān, which was for ever present in the life of the Muslims. It conveyed a rich human image, far from the absolute idealism to which later Islamic sentiment is prone in its attempts to live up to the role model embodied in the prophet Mohammed. In any case, the historical data available about the childhood and youth of Mohammed, once they are stripped

[13] "Tout personnage historique est transfiguré par la mémoire populaire en héros mythique, son histoire personnelle se transformant en histoire exemplaire," M. Eliade, *Briser le toit de la maison*, Paris, 1986, p. 316. Every historic figure is transfigured by popular memory into a mythical hero, with his personal history transformed into an exemplary history.

of the typical mythological tinge that was later added to them, are confused and negligible. We know little more about him than that he was a descendant of Hāshem, a member of the tribes of the Quraysh, who were of great symbolic and moral importance because of the role played by some of their leaders since Qusay established the status of the *kaᶜba* by receiving pilgrims there and providing them with water. The Quraysh had therefore achieved their prominence without the help of any wealth gained by trade or the dominance that the Umayyads enjoyed over Mecca and its surroundings.[14]

Mohammed was born in Mecca around 569 A.D. His father had died before his birth, and he grew up as an orphan. Like other children of the Quraysh aristocracy, he spent part of his childhood in the desert of Hawazin near al-Tā'if, where he acquired the gift of pure language. He used to visit his mother from time to time, accompanied by his nurse, and he participated in the wanderings of her people. It is also reported that he went with her to Sūq ᶜUqāz during that period. The accounts that reach us of Mohammed's biography after his mother's death on a journey back from Yathrib (Medina) become even scantier. All that remains are disconnected glimpses. His grandfather ᶜAbdul al-Muttalib took him into his care for two years, and when he died, his son Abu Tālib succeeded him as Mohammed's guardian despite his limited resources. Mohammed made several journeys to Syria, once in the company of his uncle Abu Tālib when he was about ten, and another time, on the business of Khadīja, who later became his wife, when he was about twenty. He also visited Yemen and the east of the Peninsula and perhaps even

[14] All the modern and early biographies of the prophet derive this information from Ibn Saᶜd's *Tabakat* and Ibn Hisham's *Sīra*, both of which contain only incomplete accounts that do not meet a historian's needs. See Abdullah Jnûf, *Mohammed before the Mission* (submitted for the DEA in the Department of Humanities, Manuba, 1999).

Ethiopia.[15] Although Islamic sentiment refuses to admit that as a child and youth Mohammed was a follower of his own people's religion, the laws of human society make it normal for a child—who is not yet able to think for himself—to imitate what others do and to follow them in all things, particularly religion, which is "a general and coherent interpretation of the universe, which supports and motivates the life of the society and the individuals."[16] It is quite probable that as a child Mohammed shared with his contemporaries the forms of worship that existed in their environment. This is proved by the following passage in Ibn Al Kalbi's book on idolatry: "We have been told that the Apostle of God once mentioned Al-ᶜUzza saying, 'I have offered a white sheep to Al-ᶜUzza while I was a follower of the religion of my people'."[17] Al-ᶜUzza was a Quraysh goddess, and offering sacrifices is of course one of the forms of worship practiced by the Quraysh.

[15] M. Hamidullah, "Les voyages du prophète avant l'Islam" (Journeys of the Prophet before Islam), *B.E.O*, XXIX (1997), pp. 221–230.

[16] G. Dumézil, *Mythes et dieux des indo-européens* (The Gods and Myths of the Indo-Europeans), Paris, 1992, p. 239.

[17] Hisham Ibn Al Kalbi, *The Book of Idols*, translated by Nabih Amin Faris, Princeton, NJ: Princeton University Press, 1952, p. 16. Ibn Al Kalbi adds that the Quraysh "were wont to circumambulate the Kaᶜbah and say 'By Allāt and Al-Ûzza and Manāh, the third idol besides. Verily they are the most exalted females whose intercession is to be sought'" (p. 17). This text is known as the "Satanic Verses," and Ibn Isḥāq, in his *Sira*, confirms that Mohammed participated in his people's sacrifices to the idols when he was "a young boy," The account reads as follows: "Zayd Bin 'Amr Bin Nufayl found fault in the idols and in those who worshiped them and said: they are futile, no harm or good comes from them, and he added: the Apostle (may God's blessing and peace be upon him) said: I never took blessing from an idol nor offered sacrifices again until God bestowed His message upon me." Zayd was the first to "upbraid [Mohammed] for idolatry and forbade [him] to worship idols'. Likewise, he was the first to abandon the religion of his people and abstain from eating the meat Mohammed presented to him from "the sacrifices offered to the idols."

All the available evidence confirms that Mohammed was known for his integrity, virtue and friendliness, and although he was withdrawn like most orphans, he was not unsociable.[18] His competence, his refinement, and indeed his beauty endeared him to Khadīja's heart, so that she proposed to him, and he remained faithful to the mature, strong, and dignified woman to the end of his days, even when many other women gathered around him. Their marriage, which produced many children, although the males died and only the females survived, played a decisive role in the direction taken by Mohammed's life. It provided him with psychological and emotional stability, guarded him from poverty and hardship, and enabled him, once he had been summoned by the herald from heaven, to devote himself entirely to his mission. He also found in Khadīja the moral support he needed most in times of trial, doubt, and depression. Thus, a variety of internal and external factors interacted to create Mohammed's personality and to endow him with self-confidence, the skill to persuade, and to win people's hearts and to attract them. These traits, which distinguished him right from the moment he declared his prophetic mission, played an effective part in ensuring the success of that mission despite many obstacles.

The picture of Mohammed fluctuates between praise for his ideal personal traits and the assertion that he attained his prophetic stature through divine selection (*istifa' 'ilāhi*) and not through any human predisposition. But divine selection does not necessarily conflict with human predisposition. What distinguishes the two is that divine selection is accepted on the basis of choice and faith, and cannot be inferred from rational arguments alone, while human predisposition is not subject to historical examination. That, with-

[18] The *waḥi* addresses Mohammed as follows: "Verily, thou art of a magnificent nature" (Chapter of the Pen 68/4), and continues: "For hadst thou been rough and rude of heart they would have dispersed from around thee" (Chapter of the family of Imran 3/159).

out doubt, is why Sheikh Mohammed ᶜAbduh first offered the conventional religious definition of revelation (Waḥi) as "God's disclosure to one of the prophets by, and according to, His legislative decree." He later dropped that definition and adopted another that he found more suitable: "the knowledge (ᶜirfān) a man finds within himself with the utter assurance that it has come from God, whether through an intermediary or without one."[19] If the latter is the case, this "knowledge" (ᶜirfān) cannot be acquired overnight, but must gradually develop under the influence of a number of personal, psychological, cultural, and social factors that exist around it. The acquisition of that "knowledge" involves receiving all these influences, arranging them in a unique manner, and organizing them in such a way as to reveal them at some times and conceal them at others.

What Mohammed learnt from his home surroundings and on his journeys, as well as from the Hanafites, or 'the People of the Book' ('Ahl al kītāb), provided him with topics for contemplation when he withdrew into Ghār Harā'. Some of it also reached his contemporaries, who attributed no importance to it, because it was beyond their intellectual horizons and their concerns, but in any case it constituted the material that ripened in his mind and made him realize that God had chosen him to communicate His message, first to his own people and then, through them, to all. The essence of the spirit of the universe was concentrated in him and when the revelation (Waḥi) struck him, he comprehended its meaning without intending to do so or even being prepared

[19] Mohammed ᶜAbduh, *The Theology of Unity*, translated by Ishaq Musah and Kenneth Cragg, London: George Allen and Unwin, 1966, p. 94. Mustapha ᶜAbdul Razeq adds in this respect: "it is noticeable that the popular view among Muslims is inclined towards the theologians' views in ages of intellectual stagnation and towards the views of the philosophers in ages of revival." He comments on ᶜAbduh's statement as follows: "this is none other than the philosophers' doctrine, even if its margins are decorated by the teachings of theologians" (Mustapha ᶜAbdul Rāzeq, *Religion, Revelation, and Islam*, Cairo, 1945, p. 80.).

for it. Nevertheless, the realization that God had chosen him to perform a grave mission, which he felt would bring him a great deal of trouble and hostility, had come to him gradually, and it is quite likely that when he received the command to read, he was beset by doubts, to the extent that he needed the support of his Khadîja and her cousin Waraqa bin Noufal, as the Sīra relates, without any details that would reflect the later Muslim view of woman and the association of her body with the forbidden.[20] Doubt befell him once more when the revelation ceased for a while. He was no longer certain whether the call he had heard was from God or from one of the demons that haunted the collective imagination. Priests, poets, magicians, and people subject to the influence of demons, who communicated with unseen forces and uttered words different from those of the laity (ᶜāmma), were familiar figures in Mohammed's environment. But Mohammed was no poet, magician, or priest. He was neither a sage made worldly-wise by experience and reflection, nor a reformer aspiring to bring about a small change in social relations, nor a seeker for political power over his tribe or people. He was a prophet in the style of the prophets of the Israelites, even if he was not afflicted with fainting, blackouts, epilepsy or any other form of nervous or abnormal behavior, as they were. He had revelations while sleeping or waking, and he did not speak of his own accord but by divine command. God spoke to him through one of his angels: "Verily it is the speech of a noble apostle, mighty, standing sure with the Lord of the throne, obeyed and trusty" (Chapter of the Folding Up 81/19–20). The angel is

[20] Khadīja said to him: "Rejoice, O son of my uncle, and be of good heart. Verily, by him in whose hand is Khadīja's soul, I have hope that thou wilt be the prophet of this people." Waraqa bin Naufal said: "There hath come unto him the greatest Nāmūs (meaning Gabriel) who came to Moses aforetime, and lo, he is the prophet of this people." Ibn Hisham, *The Life of Muhammad: A Translation of Ibn Ishdq's Sirat Rasul Allah*, London and New York: Oxford University Press, 1955, p. 107.

later identified in the Qur'ân in the Chapter of the Heifer (2/97) as Gabriel (Gībra-'il, i.e the strong one of God).

Thus, the speech he heard and which increased in intensity when "the faithful spirit came down with it upon [his] heart," according to the Qur'ānic expression,[21] was either the word of God conveyed in a human tongue, or possibly the word of God and the word of Mohammed at the same time.[22] It was the word of God with regard to its origin, and the word of a human being in the sense that it belonged to a specific language and was put into words and phrases dictated by the vocabulary and syntax of that language, in addition to the fact that it was embedded in an intellectual framework appropriate to Mohammed's personal education and the culture provided by the environment in which he lived. It is striking that the Muslim ᶜUlamā' (scholars) in the past did not fail to record that the revelation (Waḥi) was uttered by Omar and other companions[23] of the prophet, although they

[21] "And, verily it is a revelation from the Lord of the worlds; the faithful spirit came down with it upon thy heart, that thou shouldst be of those who warn; in plain Arabic language" (Chapter of the Poets 26/192–195) (a mainly Meccan chapter); "Say, 'Who is an enemy to Gabriel?' for he hath revealed to thy heart with God's permission" (Chapter of the Heifer 2/97). It is strange that the conservatives were enraged when a modern scholar wrote about those two verses: "The Qur'ān is entirely the word of God and, in an ordinary sense, also entirely the word of Mohammed," Fazlur Rahman, *Islam*, London: University of Chicago Press, 1966, p. 30. In this context we note Hisham Jaᶜit's opinion "that Mohammed received the revelation (waḥi) passively," *The Revelation, the Qur'ān, and the Prophecy*, Beirut, Dar 'Attalyᶜa, 1999, p. 70. This opinion is not consistent with the logic of the analysis of the prophecy and the revelation in the rest of that book.

[22] "We have only made it easy for thy tongue that thou mayest thereby give glad tidings to the pious, and warn thereby a contentious people" (Chapter of Mary 19/97).

[23] See Jalāl Ad-dān as-Suyutā, *al-Itqān*, the tenth type: parts of the Qur'ān that were reported by the prophet's companions. Al-Zamakhshari mentions in his *Kashāf*, Beirut, Dar al-Maᶜrifa, v1, pp. 299–310, instances in which "the ijtihādāt (personal reasonings) of ᶜUmar corresponded to God's Sharᶜ." See also Abdelmajid Sharfi, "Fi Qirā'at al-Turāth al-Dīnī" (A Reading of Religious Tradition) in: *Labanat*, Tunis, 1994, pp. 113–129.

insisted on its divine source. To resolve the apparent contradiction, one must not examine the parts and details of what Mohammed might have known and what occupied his mind and the minds of his companions. The lesson lies in the unique synthesis in which the elements unite in such a way as to advance the end intended by Divine Providence. The material circumstances and human elements would have a value of their own only if they lacked a hidden dimension expressing something that transcends history, and if their conditions and structures were not directed towards an ultimate thought. For what is faith but having confidence in such a wisdom and attempting to be saturated with the enthralling 'manifest signs' (al bayināt) in the same manner as a man who craves sunlight exposes himself to it, ignoring the concerns of the physicist, who analyses its components, and paying no heed to the burns and strokes he may suffer if he fails to exercise due care and caution.

Although theologians (al Mutakalīmūn) do not usually elaborate on the nature and process of revelation—insisting as they do on the two notions of 'responsibility or obligation under religious law' (taklīf) and 'cult' or 'service to God' (ᶜibāda), and focusing their attention on proving the ability of prophets to work miracles—the notion established in Islamic literature, and irreplaceable in the Muslim mind, is that both the word and the meaning were revealed to the prophet. Nevertheless, one of the views reported by as-Suyuti in *Al 'Itqān* is that "Gabriel came down with the meanings and he (may God's blessing and peace be upon him) knew these meanings and expressed them in the language of the Arabs."[24] as-Suyutī finds no blasphemy or apostasy in such a statement. In fact, this view is the closest to modern rationality, and may perhaps be a suitable starting point for a new

[24] as-Suyutī adds: "the speaker of this took the surface meaning of God's saying: 'the faithful spirit came down with it upon thy heart'," (Chapter of the Poets 26/192). Thus it seems that the ancients were more open-minded than many of our contemporaries.

progressive thought that does not clash with the revelation (Waḥi) and is unfettered by the theories inherited on the pretext of the consensus formed around them. This progressive thought will preserve the transcendent divine dimension of the Qur'ân without any reification, as well as its natural human dimension with its historicity and relativity; nor will it separate the two dimensions and either exclude one or emphasize it at the expense of the other, as does the "Sunni" conception, which deprives the prophet of his will and his faculties.[25] Is it not the purpose of the prophetic mission to give everybody a share in the experience of the divine, which the prophet underwent at a superior level? How could the modern Muslim be forbidden to try to explain, by means of the knowledge available to him, what the revelation (Waḥi) left out? And yet he is even forbidden to contemplate what the ancients allowed themselves to contemplate and interpret in accordance with their own mental frame of reference.

The Muslim philosophers have tried to explain the phenomenon of prophethood (nubuwwa) on the basis of the conceptions available in their culture. Al-Kindī, for example, suggests that the knowledge of prophets is attained "without any pain or effort or intention, not through the ploys of mathematics and logic, and not in time, but with the will of

[25] The components of the conception that has been established in Muslim consciousness concerning the method of revelation are discussed in the books of Hadīth, the books of Speculative Theology, and the books of Qur'ānic sciences. See Mustapha ᶜAbed Al Razeq, *Religion, Revelation, and Islam*, Cairo, 1945, quoted above; Fazlur Rahman, *Prophecy in Islam. Philosophy and Orthodoxy*, London, 1958, who analyzed the theories of Avicenna as well as those of Fārābī, Ibn Hazm, Al Shahrastani, Ibn Taymia, and Ibn Khaldūn, relating to prophethood (nubuwwa). See also Ali Mabrouk, *Prophecy*, Cairo, 1993, who chronicles the phenomenon of prophecy before Islam on the basis of modern sources and then turns to the Islamic theological essays, but only dares to express his opinion about the nature of Mohammed's prophecy in a timid and indirect way in one of the margins, p. 100.

the Almighty to purify their souls and to enlighten them with certitude, with His support, His inspiration, and His command."[26] Al Fārābī says: "It is not impossible, then, that when a man's faculty of representation reaches its utmost perfection he will receive in his waking life from the Active Intellect present and future particulars or their imitations in the form of sensibles, and receive the imitations of the transcendent intelligibles and the other glorious existents and see them"[27] It is evident from these attempts that the philosophers aim at rationalizing the phenomenon of prophethood, which is central to religion, and at transcending the naďve view based on faith, but that the only support they can find for their conception is provided by notions such as purification, representation, and the ultimate link with the Active Intellect or the spiritual connection of the human faculty of reason with the celestial souls—a connection that allows reason to look upon the reflections of the temporal events in the celestial souls in the same manner as images are seen on the surface of a mirror.

If anything, this would show that not all Muslims in the past were satisfied or convinced by the prevalent conception, but the majority were not ready to accept the consequences of admitting the actual role of the prophet in the delivery of the mission. They preferred to assume that his role was a passive one: God spoke with a human tongue and the angel listened, or God spoke and the angel translated into Arabic, so that the Apostle received the revelation from the angel and passed it on mechanically, without in any way interfering in the formulation of what he was commanded to convey. What led to this conception was above all the Qur'ānic use of the expression 'word of God'. As we shall see soon,

[26] Al Kindi, *Rasā'il al kindi al falsāfia,* (Al Kindi's Philosophical Treatise), edited by Abou Reeda, Cairo, 1950, p. 373.

[27] Al Fārābi, *On the Perfect State,* translated by Richard Walzer, New York: Oxford University Press, 1985, p. 224.

this expression means two different things: on the one hand the divine, transcendent quality that cannot be captured in human language without the risk of reification, and on the other hand the prophetic mission that originates from God, but that is framed in time and space, so that it can be conveyed by a human being who fulfills all the conditions of humanity: he thinks, feels, imagines, hopes, despairs, and is susceptible to contentment, anger and all the other human emotions. The expression "word of God" was thought to have one specific meaning, without taking into consideration the limitations of language when conveying abstract concepts and the fact that the same term can often carry several different meanings.

The belief in holiness or a magical touch (in the sense of Max Weber) dominated the world in which Mohammed lived, as indeed it dominated humanity as a whole until the seventeenth century.[28] Moreover, the mythical mentality, which is characterized by intuition and imitation, prevailed in many peoples' and many cultures' way of thinking at the time. Thus, it is not surprising to find traces of these two phenomena in Mohammed's message to his people and to the Muslims in general.

Whether we consider this matter from a perspective based on pure faith or from an objective historical point of view, it means that God addresses people with something that they can understand, or else His revelation would be in vain. It also means that the prophet had to draw on what was available and prevalent in his own environment.[29] Nevertheless,

[28] Cf. Lucien Febvre, Le problème de l'incroyance au XVIème s. *La religion de Rabelais*, Paris, 1968 (1ère ed: 1942).

[29] Nasr Hāmid Abou Zayd says: "The Qur'ān describes itself as a message, and a message represents a connection through a code or a linguistic system between a sender and a recipient. Since the sender in the case of the Qur'ān cannot be subjected to scientific study, it is only natural that the key approach to the study of the Qur'ānic text should be based on reality and culture," *Mafhūm an-Naṣṣ* (The Concept of the Text), Beirut and Casablanca, 1996, pp. 24.

all these elements were employed, as we shall see, in a manner that transcended the limited historical circumstances, in order to achieve objectives that may have been beyond what the contemporaries of the mission were ready to accept.

We can therefore understand the Prophet's lack of reserve in adopting many views advanced by his companions and incorporating them into the revelation (Waḥi). For example:

- Barā' bin Marur was probably the first to have turned towards Kaᶜbah instead of Syria, before the Qîbla was redirected to Kaᶜbah by the revelation (Waḥi).

- When Mohammed first came to the Madîna, the Muslims gathered round him for prayer without being summoned. In due course he resolved to "use a trumpet like that of the Jews who used it to summon to prayer. Then he disliked the idea and ordered a clapper to be made, so it was duly fashioned to be beaten when the Muslims were to pray."[30] Finally, he adopted Abdullah bin Zayd bin Thaᶜlaba's suggestion—or vision—and asked Bīlāl to call for prayers in, or very close to, the manner that became established later.

- After the raid on Quraysh in Nakhla during the sacred month, Abdullah bin Jaḥsh was the first to set apart one-fifth of the booty for the Prophet and divide the rest among those who had participated in the raid. In later justifying fighting in the sacred month "on the basis of what Abdullah had done with the booty of that caravan," and in confirming the division of the booty by the commander of the expedition, the Waḥi most probably followed a convention of the pre-Islamic society, which distinguished the leader of the tribe from the rest of the raiders.[31] The writers of the Sīra (the

[30] Ibn Hisham, *op.cit.*, p. 236.

[31] *Ibid.*, p. 286. This account further relates that when Mohammed sent out the commander of the expedition he "wrote a letter for him and ordered him not to look at it until he had journeyed for two days" (p. 287). This indicates that Mohammed could write. On the other hand, it can be understood from another account, on p. 199. and subsequent pages, that Abou Umāma Asᶜad b. Zurāra was "the first to bring the Muslims together"

Prophet's biography) found nothing to criticize in this and similar incidents.

Accordingly, we can understand what we are told about past prophets and bygone nations in the Qur'ān, which retains, with strong emphasis and in almost the same form, many things that had significance in the minds of people at that time, for example the punishment that awaited those who denied the prophet's call for monotheism and the necessity of denying the pagan religions of the forefathers, as stated in the account of the prophets in the Chapter of Hûd. Mohammed was accused of having received these accounts and stories from a foreign, non-Arab person.[32] The aim of this accusation was to disavow the prophecy and to deny Mohammed's special relationship with God, through which he learnt what he did not know. The revelation's answer to that was: "These are stories of the unseen which we revealed to thee; thou didst not know them, thou nor thy people before this" (Chapter of Hûd 11/49); "Thou couldst not recite before this any book, nor write with thy right hand" (Chapter of the Spider 29/48). As Mohammed did not know the unseen,[33] the revelation was his source of knowledge. Revela-

---

in the Medina, so that the Apostle had adopted what b. Zurāra had initiated.

[32] "We knew that they said, 'It is only some mortal who teaches him.'—The tongue of him they lean towards is barbarous, and this is plain Arabic." (Chapter of the Bee 16/103). See also the many verses which refer to him being accused of forgery and innovation: "They say, 'Old folks' tales, which he has got written down while they are dictated to him morning and evening" (Chapter of the Discrimination 25/5); "Or will they say he has forged against God a lie?" (Chapter of Counsel 42/24).

[33] "Say, 'I do not say to you, mine are the treasures of God, nor that I know the unseen; I do not say to you I am an angel—if I follow aught but what I am inspired with" (Chapter of the Cattle 6/50); "Say, 'I cannot control profit or harm for myself, save what God will. If I knew the unseen I should surely have much that is good, nor would evil touch me" (Chapter of Al Aarāf 7/188).

tion is the exceptional state in which consciousness is lost and all acquired faculties are suspended, bringing to light what is buried in the depth of the unconscious by an extraordinary power that the prophet cannot ward off or control. It discloses in a very special way the specific representations of what the divine will dictates to him. In other words, it is a unique disclosure of the ultimate, the infinite, and the metaphysical in a manner that no ordinary man with his limited intellectual abilities can achieve. I repeat that at this level the perspective based on faith does not contradict that based on science or knowledge. For the two perspectives differ only with regard to the origin of that extraordinary power, and not with regard to its essence. The first perspective ascribes it to God, while the second adopts a phenomenological explanation. The first answers the questions "from where?" and "how?," while the second is content with answering the "how?" alone. But both agree on a very essential point, which is Mohammed's sincerity or his confidence that he is not expressing his personal views but communicating exclusively what God has revealed to him.[34] The method of modern research is not satisfied with interpreting history on the basis of its objective, neutral components alone, but, rather, links those components with the universal, and acknowledges that events have a possible transcendent meaning that goes beyond sensual perception.

In all cases, these stories and accounts serve a function which is not denied by revelation and which is "establishing the prophet's heart."[35] In modern terms, revelation gives the prophet confidence in himself and in the validity of his message. For, in his confrontation with non-believers, he has nothing but God as his witness that what he receives is sent

[34] "Say, It is not for me to change it of my own accord" (Chapter of Jonah 10/15), "This Qu'rān could not have been devised by any besides God" (Chapter of Jonah 10/37).

[35] "And all that we relate to thee of the stories of the apostles is what will establish thy heart" (Chapter of Hûd 11/120).

by God.[36] That is why the revelation tells him: "Let there be no straitness in thy breast" (Chapter of Al Aarâf 7/2), and why it is stressed, on several occasions, that the revelation received by Mohammed is similar to that received by the other apostles before him. There is no distinction between the inspiration they received and the revelation that was exclusively disclosed to him. Furthermore, the same expressions are used in relation to all the apostles without any distinctions (brought down, descended, sent to you, revealed to you, recited, chose, warned, brought forth, herald, preach, the book, furqān, wisdom, manifest signs, the words of God, the message of God, certitude, the prophet, the apostle).[37] The fate of Mohammed's message was different from that of the message of Jesus and Moses, since the Old Testament (the Torah) was only recorded many centuries after the death of Moses and after the Babylonian captivity. Similarly, the New Testament (the Gospel) was recorded in several different versions, although the church only retained four, in which the words of Jesus merged with accounts of his life. On the other hand, Mohammed's message was written down soon after his death and the message he conveyed was separated from his biography. That is why what was recorded of the two former missions lacks the guarantees of validity present in the Holy Qur'ān. However, this does not imply any essential difference in the quality of the three missions, or in the problems that arise when dealing with them, particularly once they were transformed from the oral type to the written, from Qur'ān[38] to scripture or text.

[36] "Or do they say, 'He has forged it?' Say, 'If I have forged ye cannot obtain for me aught from God; He knows best what ye utter concerning it; He is witness enough between me and you, and He is forgiving and merciful'" (Chapter of El 'Ahqāf 46/8), and other verses.

[37] Chapter of the Heifer 2/53, 89, 92, 97, 159, 163, 213, 251, 253; Chapter of Imrān's Family 3/48, 184; Chapter of Women 4/163; Chapter of the Table 5/48; Chapter of Al Aarāf 7/144; Chapter of Jonah 10/47. Review: Mohammad Fouad ʿAbed Albaqi, *Al Mu'jam li 'Alfāẕh Al Qur'ān*, Cairo.

[38] The word "Qur'ān" in Arabic comes from the root "Qara'a," which

How many times did the Apostle remind his listeners that he was not bringing them any novelties but merely continuing in the path of earlier apostles, those of the Israelites, starting from Abraham, and those of the Arab region, such as Saleḥ[39]? He constantly stressed that what he was bringing them "confirmed" what they already possessed and what the Israelites had already received.[40] And did God not write, for the mission of Moses, "upon tablets an admonition concerning everything and a detailing of everything" (Chapter of Al 'Aᶜarāf 7/145)? Can we still be amazed after all that, if it is said that the essence of the missions of all apostles is pure monotheism, and that what they all call for is charity, benevolence, and the performance of good deeds, just as they call for the rejection of polytheism, arrogance, and evil in general? We do not need to elaborate on this, for it is known to the elite as well as to the ordinary people that the belief in the apostles and the prophets who preceded Mohammed is an indisputable issue among Muslims, even if some of them try to discriminate between the apostles and to declare one of them to be superior, remembering that the Qur'ān mentioned this superiority although it did not elaborate on it. What the Qur'ān specifically does not say is that Mohammed's mission annuls the earlier ones. His mission was considered ascendant over its predecessors, but ascendancy does not mean annulment!

Thus, we realize that the new message is an extension of the previous monotheistic messages. It contains elements from the culture of seventh-century Mecca, of Ḥījāz and the Peninsula, and of the whole Middle East. Nor should it be

---

means 'read'. Thus the word Qur'ān in itself refers to an oral message (recitation), which is read out and heard. (Translator's note)

[39] The Apostle said, when the daughter of Khalid b. Sinān Al ᶜAbsi came to him: "This is the daughter of a prophet whom his people lost," Al Jahiz, *Al Hayawān*, Beirut, 1979, p. 477.

[40] Chapter of the Heifer 2/89, 97; Chapter of the table 5/48; Chapter of the cattle 6/92; Chapter of Jonah 10/37.

expected to be any different, since it is addressed to humanity and to specific people. It is obvious that its references to the jinn, the descent from heaven, the role of Satan and the demons,[41] the angels, the flood,[42] Noah's age, and all the other mythical features, which seem very strange and distant from today's notions and conceptions, are derived from those cultural elements, and there are many other instances of the strange and the extraordinary in the new message, which no longer have the same effect on the minds of our contemporaries.[43]

However, the existence of these elements must not blind us to the other side of this mission, which it also had in common with earlier missions: its opposition to the prevalent values and beliefs. The Mohammedan mission departed from what already existed in order to change it and to point it in a different direction from what people were accustomed to and satisfied with. Although it took the conventional into consideration, it did not linger on it or expand it. If these missions had not challenged the views, beliefs, and morals that people had received from their forefathers and that had become established in their minds as axiomatic, and if, furthermore, they had not tried to curb the existing financial

[41] It is fit to note here that from the perspective of the mission, evil spirits are merely creatures of God, and it is not asked of Muslims to worship them or curry favor with, as later became the case according to popular belief.

[42] In this respect, we note that the discovery of the text of *the Epic of Gilgamesh* caused great confusion in the Jewish and Christian circles at that time, for it turned out in the year 1872 that the discovered texts contain an account similar to that of the flood in the book of Genesis (Chapter VI-VIII).

[43] See Wahid Assaᶜfi, *Al ᶜAjīb wal Gharīib fi Kutub Tafsīr Al Qur'ān, Tafsīr Ibn Kathīr 'Unmuzajan,* (The Strange and Marvelous in the Books of Qur'ānic Exegesis, the Exegesis of Ibn Kathir as a Specimen), which explains Mohammad ᶜAbduh's denial that the Qur'ān aims at recording history through its narratives. This is what Mohammad Ahmad Khalaf tried to prove in his dissertation on *Al Fan Al Kasasī fil Qur'ān al Karīm,* (The Art of Narrative in the Holy Qur'ān), Cairo, 1957.

and moral sectarian interests, it would be impossible to explain the strong resistance encountered by Mohammed and the other apostles.[44] At the same time it was precisely what was new and original in these missions that justified their existence and held the secret of their prevalence and endurance. It is also what still justifies people's belief in them, despite all the different races and circumstances, as long as tyranny and injustice exist in this world.

It is only natural that inherited conceptions, values, morals, and interests do not suddenly fade away with the coming of the prophetic mission. They bend like reeds in the wind. They do not break or die, but lie low, waiting for the storm to pass, so that they may rise again in a different guise. In particular, they try to exploit people's urgent needs, in order to regain what they have lost. They may succeed in that in varying degrees, but their success will be at the expense of the higher aim of the mission; it would in fact mean a relapse, a sham, and a retreat.

[44] Prophethood is that common outlet. However, it is always a unique phenomenon, by means of which a minority of people aspire to escape the injustices that constitute the social order in its progress towards radicalism, which is a product of 'fidelity'. But, prophethood is not only a guard against injustices. It is a critical rejecter like "spring in the trees of the spiritual meadows." J. Lambert, *Le dieu distribué* (The Distributed God), Paris, 1996, p. 78.

CHAPTER THREE

THE CHARACTERISTICS OF THE MOHAMMEDAN MISSION

Before embarking on the study of the outcome of the Mohammedan Mission, we must first consider some of its exegeses, in order to rectify them and to place them in their proper context. This will provide us with a solid base on which to proceed. I am well aware that religion–any religion–is not identical with the form in which it is manifested in history, but this does not preclude a historical study of religions. Moreover, it does not cancel the differentiation between "open" religions and "closed" religions, to use the terminology of the French philosopher Henri Bergson, nor that between the original religious call and the different ways of embracing religion. These are usually overlaid with rituals that perform certain social tasks fundamentally aimed at strengthening the bonds between individuals and imposing a minimal standard of discipline. When such rituals prevail, various alliances gain ascendancy over the truth, and the necessity of harmonizing the different constituents of society takes precedence over the sincerity of conscience. That is why taking a step back and considering the nature of the Mohammedan mission may assist us in clearing up the obscurities and in learning to use the terminology in its original sense and not in the one that it later acquired under a variety of influences.

I should start by emphasizing the oral quality of the poetic address, for–unlike the prophet's contemporaries, who saw him, listened to him, and accompanied him for a longer or shorter period, but like all the Islamic generations since—we lack any direct knowledge of the particulars of that address, that is, the exact circumstances surrounding it, the individual or individuals concerned, and the intended or stated purpose, let alone the conditions specific to each Qur'ānic verse (āya) or group of verses, and to each Sūra. It is true that Qur'ānic Studies include what is known as "the occasions or causes of revelation" (*Asbāb Annuzūl*), but the prophet's contemporaries did not pay much attention to these occasions since they lived through them and experienced them at first hand. It was the later generations who sought to learn about them. Moreover, these "occasions" were recorded in a later period, at least two or three generations later, and then only in part. Thus, it is quite natural that they were subject to additions and led to confusion.[45]

We have also lost the sense of the tone in which the prophetic address was delivered, suggesting satisfaction or anger, friendly advice, warning or rebuke, none of which can be conveyed by a written record of the words alone. Even a simple, everyday expression like 'Good Morning'—depending on the different tones in which it is uttered—can indicate whether the speaker is merely performing the duty of greeting as dictated by convention, truly delighted to meet the person concerned, or annoyed about some delay, blunder, or slackness. Facial expressions and inflections of the voice accompanying speech can also be ways of conveying meaning. These examples are enough to make us realize the great importance of the circumstances surrounding speech, which are lost when speech is written down and when—like all recorded texts, and in particular fundamental religious ones—it is subjected to a myriad of exegeses, which often contradict each other, as a result of differences in views, interests, moods and mentalities. The contradictions are eventually

[45] See Naṣr Hāmid Abū Zayd, *Mafhūm an-Naṣṣ* (The Concept of the Text), pp. 108–115.

resolved in the context of one tradition or of several competing traditions struggling to disqualify each other and to assert an exclusive claim to the correct exegesis.

In fact, the term 'Qur'ān' applies only to the prophet's oral address to his contemporaries. As for the material that was arranged in a specific order and recorded "between two covers" after the prophet's death, it is common knowledge that the prophet's companions themselves initially disagreed about the legitimacy of this compilation, since it had been neither carried out nor commanded by him. That is why Abū Bakr rejected ᶜUmar b. Al Khattāb's opinion concerning this issue until "God enlightened him" on the ᶜUmar's initiative. The companions even hesitated about what name to give to this new phenomenon, before it was finally settled that it should be called al Muṣḥaf (codex), following the example known to some of them from Al-Habasha (Ethiopia).[46]

The different versions of the Qur'ānic manuscript were codified or canonized as a result of a political decision during the reign of ᶜUthmān, who declared one Muṣḥaf the official one and burnt all the others, fearing that the Muslims might become embroiled in disputes over their book like the Christians and the Jews.[47] Similarly, during the rule of Mar-

[46] See for example Jalāl Ad-dīn as-Suyutī, *al-'Itqān*. In a lecture given on May 15, 2000, Dr. Mohammed al Tālibī explained that the Qur'ān was recorded on vellum and not in the primitive ways commonly reported, and he cited in evidence the verse: "Consider the mountain, and the Book written in an out-stretched vellum" (The Mountain (at-tūr) 52/1-3). However, the sūra of The Mountain is entirely Meccan and cannot therefore refer to the whole of the Qur'ān or the *Muṣḥaf;* nor is the book mentioned in it in a material sense, as we shall see later.

[47] Ibn Abī Dāwūd narrates in his book *al Maṣāḥif,* that when the "muṣḥaf" was first brought to ᶜUthmān, ᶜUthmān said: "It raises suspicions of solecisms, but the Arab tongue will correct it," Cairo edition, 1937, p. 32. He also mentions Ali's question addressed to those who rebelled against ᶜUthmān: "What is it that makes you bear a grudge?," and their reply: "He erased the book of God Almighty," p. 36. Al-Tabari, in his history, reports the rebels' answer as follows: "The Qur'ān was many books, and he (ᶜUthmān) left them only one," Cairo editions, 1970, v. 4, p. 347.

wān b. al-Ḥakām the musḥaf of Ḥafṣa—one of the prophet's wives—was burnt. As much as historians regret the loss of this original manuscript, they cannot but admit that unifying and codifying the Muṣḥaf had many undeniable advantages. Had it not been for this codification, the integration of Muslims through one and the same book might have been delayed. This delay would have carried with it all the possibilities of much graver secessions and divisions than those that occurred at the end of ᶜUthmān's rule, particularly because the political authority is bound to be involved in all disputes, given that it owes its existence to religion, and that it derives its legitimacy from it, influences it, and is influenced by it, whether negatively or positively.

The logical conclusion that imposes itself in view of the historical reality is that the 'Dhikr', which God promised to preserve, is the meaning and not the circumstances; it is the content of the mission: its lessons and warnings, its advice and guidance. The mission is the content that it delivered and not the language in which it was formulated. It is not merely the words and expressions that were recorded at a certain time, ascribed to a specific people, and characterized by their grammar and their turns of phrase, which, in principle, does not differ from one language to the next. The prophet himself allowed his companions to recite the verses ('ayāt) they had memorized in different ways, and he considered all the versions acceptable. It was some of the companions who insisted on the reading they had heard from the prophet, emphasizing the singularity of the recital and believing that any plurality was a distortion of the word of God.[48] When the Qur'ān challenged the unbelievers to pro-

---

There is no doubt that ᶜUthmân's initiative was of great symbolic significance, and it explains the resentment towards him better than any of the many reasons retained in collective memory, such as his reliance on his relatives.

[48] See the account of ᶜUmar b. al-Khattāb and Hishām b. Ḥakīm in *Saḥīḥ al Bukhārī*, the book of the virtues of the Qur'ān: the Qur'ān was revealed to

duce ten sūras, or even one sūra, on a par with its own, it was not because the Qur'ān was inimitable in its rhetoric, but rather because it was drawn from a divine source inaccessible to ordinary people and only revealed to God's prophets and apostles. There is no doubt that the Qur'ānic style is a distinct, refined, and unique one. Every reader or listener can sense its exceptionality. Now, every unique work of art, whether a piece of poetry or prose, a painting, a sculpture, or a musical composition, is inimitable in its own way. It cannot be recreated perfectly, even though it is man-made. All one can do in the face of a great masterpiece–if one has the necessary talent and ability–is to attempt an imitation, but imitation always degrades the original. For, if one were able to create a true equal, one would in fact have produced a new masterpiece, and that would no longer be an imitation. As for the unbelievers who were challenged to produce sūras on a par with those of the Qur'ān, how could they possibly possess the powers of a prophet? With the exception of Muᶜtazila, who early on believed in the *Ṣirfa*[49] (prevention), i.e. the idea that the unique style of the Qur'ān cannot be

---

be recited in seven different ways, and the prophet himself allowed different readings. In fact it was his permission to Abdullah b. Abi Saᶜd b. al Sarḥ, one of the scribes of the revelation, to replace "mighty, wise" with "knowing, wise" and "the unbelievers" with "the unjust," and his saying that "All is right," that caused this scribe to doubt and forsake his Islamic faith. See Ibn al Athīr, *Usd al Ghaba*, Cairo, 1970, 3/359, Al Balādhurī, *Futūḥ al Buldān*, Cairo, 1932, p. 359. It is related that Abdullah bin Masᶜud asked a man to recite: "Surely the tree of the Zuqqum, is the food of the sinful (al Athīm)" (The Drought 43/44). The man said: "the food of the orphan (al yatīm)" Bin Masᶜūd corrected the man, but he still could not pronounce the word correctly. When bin Masᶜud asked him whether he could say the immoral (*al fājir*) and the man said yes, bin Masᶜud told him to do so. Jalāl Ad-dīn as-Suyutī, *al-'Itqan*. Sixteen. On the flexibility that distinguishes the oral religious address from the written, see Goody, J., *La logique de l'écriture*, Paris, 1986, p. 21.

[49] See Van Ess, J., "Une lecture à rebours de l'histoire du mu'tazilisme" (A Reverse Reading of the History of Mu'tazila) , in: *R.E.I.*, LXVI, Fasc. 2, 1978, pp. 185–194.

imitated by humans not because of its language but because God had made people's hearts incapable of bringing forth its equal, most Muslim thinkers attributed the inimitability of the Qur'ān to its composition. The view that the inimitability of the Qur'ān lay in its extraordinary style and form—what has been known since Abd al-Qāhir al-Jurgānī as *an-nazm*—can be explained by the desire of the majority of Muslim thinkers to infer the prophet's sincerity, and the core of the doctrine, on a basis that can be subjected to experimentation. For it is not possible to infer any arguments based on the divine source of the Qur'ān by reason: they can only be believed or denied, but this would demolish the foundations of the theologians' profession, at least as it was practiced in earlier times.

It does no harm to point out in this context that the memories of the Qur'ān in the hearts and minds and the guarantees that most Muslims cite in respect of its codification and recording—which were equally lacking when the missions of Moses and Jesus were recorded generations or centuries after their eras—are paralleled among the Jews, and in particular the orthodox, with regard to the Torah. This is the case despite many excavations in Palestine and serious historical studies explaining that the events related by the Torah have no basis in history and are a later "ideological" construct made up by the Jews after their capture by Nebuchadnezzar and their exile to Babylon in the sixth century B.C. By the time they had returned from exile they were faced with a new world that was wider and richer than their old narrow and closed one. Thus they employed some of the "fundamental myths" circulating throughout the region for the composition of their own religious texts,[50] while also insisting on the rituals and prohibitions mentioned in the books of the Torah and in the interpretations of the rabbis. A

[50] See Herzog, Z., "Deconstructing the Walls of Jericho" in *Ha'aretz*, 19/10/1999, pp. 1–8. Françoise Smyth Florentin has supplied proof of this in many of her studies.

similar situation obtains with Christians and the teachings of the official church. Some of these, in particular the fundamentalist Protestants, still believe that all the details mentioned in the Holy Bible are literally true, from the history of the world and the origin of man (who, they insist, first appeared a few thousand and not five million years ago, as modern science teaches)[51] to the simplest rules of conduct.

The term "book" is a very ambiguous one. The common view is that a book is something written on stone, bone, papyrus or any other appropriate material surface. The Qur'ān does not refer to this meaning at all when it mentions either the book in general or the book of God, nor when it refers to the written book (*al kitāb al masṭūr*), or the book that descended to Mohammed and the other prophets and apostles, or to the "right books" in the "pure pages," recited by the prophet[52] or the followers of the book (*ahl al kitāb*). What is meant by all these uses of the term "book" is not the material object that one can touch and copy, open and close, and put aside, but rather the content that God instructed his prophets to convey to humanity. It is the message in which He shows them the way to piety in all its forms and directs them to what is good for their lives now and hereafter. This view is strongly supported by the fact that the term 'book' was used even before Mohammed had received the whole of the Qur'ān, which descended in several parts, separated by varying periods of time. We must not forget that the role of reading and writing differs from one era and one society to

[51] Of course, like the ignorant among the Muslims, they reject the notion of evolution, about which one of the most prominent contemporary scientists writes: "it must be admitted that all animals existing on this earth today are descendants of the same earlier organism that existed six million years ago and already possessed a battery of genes," F. Jacob, "Les surprises du 'bricolage moleculaire' ," in *Le Monde*, 4/1/2000, p. 14.

[52] The chapter of the Clear Evidence (Bayyina) (98/3-2). See also the chapter of 'He frowned' (ᶜAbasa) (80/11-16): "Nay! Surely it is an eminence. So let him who pleases mind it, in honored books, exalted purified in the hands of scribes, noble virtuous."

another. Reading, for the Arabs, was an oral and public function, as it was for the ancient Greeks and others. One man spoke, while the others listened and discussed what he had said. It was not until the second century after the hijra that the book as a material object became available as a result of the development of the paper industry and the spread of books in the material sense, due to influences from China. Even then it was not possible to depend on inscribed or etched writings because Arabic writing in the era of the prophet was devoid of diacritical signs. Furthermore, it is quite an overstatement to claim that the Qur'ān alone is the book of God. For, according to the logic of revelation, it is only the "version" that considers the affairs of people in Mohammed's own time within the mental framework of that specific era.

The same applies to divine speech. All those who have any idea of the history of Islamic thought are aware of the violent disputes that took place in the Abbasid era among theologians, jurists, and traditionists (specialists in Prophetic tradition or ḥadīth). In the third century of the hijra, in the times of al-Ma'mūn, al-Muᶜtasim, al-Wāthik, and al-Mutawakil, and later in the fifth century during the reign of ᶜAbd al Qadir, the political authority interfered in these disputes and sided with whichever party best served its interests. These disputes were about whether or not the Qur'ān was the "created" or "uncreated" word of God,[53] in addition to the distinction made by the Ashᶜarites between psychological and articulated speech. The Muslims at that time recognized the difficulty of proving the divine source of the Mohammedan mission without falling into the faults of 'reification' and 'assimilation', but they failed to take into consideration the fact that the revelation at that level was compelled to use

[53] In relation to this, see Madelung, W., "The Origins of the Controversy Concerning the Creation of the Koran," in *Orientala Hispanica. Sive studia F. M. Pareja...*, Brill, 1974, vol. 1, pp. 504–525; and also: Fahmi Jadᶜan, *al Miḥna: al Baḥth fī jadaliyyāt ad-dīn wa as-siyāsa fī al-Islam*, Amman, 1989.

human concepts to indicate transcendental truths. The Qur'ān itself refers to these truths as ungraspable, so how is it possible for a material vessel (words) to contain them? "Say: If the sea were ink for the words of my Lord, the sea would surely be consumed before the words of my Lord are exhausted" (The Cave 18/109).[54] Furthermore, they did not realize that what is meant by the Qur'ān is not only the actual words uttered by Mohammed but also, and more essentially, the content God wanted to convey and which He describes as follows: "Most surely it is an honored Qur'ān, in a book that is protected; none shall touch it but the purified ones; a revelation by the Lord of the worlds" (The Great Event 56/77-80). The 'analogical juxtaposition of the absent to the present' (*qiyās al-ghā'ib ᶜala al-shāhid*) is what caused them, here as on many other occasions, to succumb to the fallacy of projecting the human onto the transcendent, thus forcibly subjecting the transcendent to necessarily limited predicaments. It also led them to reification, in addition to other factors that will be discussed later.

To avoid the critical situation which results from confusing abstract metaphysical transcendent truths with concrete human truths, and from considering what is true of the former as being entirely true of the latter, we must not overlook the technique adopted by the *waḥī.* It is a technique based on the use of symbols, metaphors, similes, signs, and allusions, to enable humans to comprehend the purpose behind the revelation and to respond to it. Moreover, we should not be seduced by the characteristics of the mythical address, nor consider them as essentially belonging to the conceptual

[54] Compare to the saying attributed by the philosopher Levinas to a Jewish priest: "If all the seas were ink and all the streams were pens, if the sky and the earth were all paper, and if all humans practiced the art of writing, they would never deplete the Torah I have memorized, whereas the Torah itself is not diminished by more than the amount of ink carried at the tip of the pen" Levinas, E., *Difficile liberté*, 2nd ed., Paris, 1976, p. 48.

sphere, as did the Qur'ānic exegetes who attempted to divide what is composite (*mujmal*), to spell out what is only alluded to, and to translate symbols in general into concrete historical events. We must also permanently keep in mind not the circumstantial commands and prohibitions that relate to the requirements of the time, place and conditions accompanying the mission, but rather the purposes and intents lying behind it. The recognition of the inconsistencies and contradictions of these commands and prohibitions, which aim at direction and guidance, is nothing new. The ancients tried to overcome them through the concept of abrogation (*naskh*). However, this concept is meaningless unless it accepts, contrary to the fundamentalists' view, the necessity of accounting for the new circumstances arising at the time of the *waḥī* and after.

In this essential issue, the solution with which the Muslims contented themselves in the second century of the hijra—the period when jurisprudence (*fiqh*) emerged as a major concern (at least for scholars), when the state organized the life of society on the basis of religion, and when the Qur'ān was recorded—was to adhere to the literariness of the text. For many centuries, the Muslims imagined this solution to be a requirement of religion, regardless of its many weaknesses, such as the preference of one Qur'ānic verse over another, the arbitrariness of this choice, and the specific exegesis involved in it, in addition to the fact that the basis of the 'juridical prescriptions or judgments' (aḥkām) in fact consisted of āḥād[55] accounts, prevailing customs, and reported precedents, rather than Qur'ānic verses.

This solution only began to diminish and lose its intuitive quality in the modern age, as a result of the rapid and crucial changes that occurred in the Islamic communities. The modern views may be divided into four main stances:

[55] The "āḥād" are prophetic traditions or accounts that go back to a single authority.

1. The first is the stance defended by most religious scholars of a traditional mindset, and it is a projection of the solution adopted by Muslims before the changes that have occurred in modern Muslim societies. It is generally characterized by the preservation of the inherited traditional system at the theoretical level but with an implicit consent to infringe it at the practical level. The adherents of this stance believe in the necessity of obeying the 'guardian in charge' (*walī al amr*) even if he is unjust, and yielding to the situational law he promulgates, even if it has only a tenuous connection with jurisprudence or none at all. Although these scholars cling to the traditional system, they fail to recognize the function it served in its own time and to realize that the conditions and concerns of the present are very different from those of the past. Many of them pursue personal and factional interests, which may be legitimate, but as a result of which religion nevertheless becomes a mere cover for those interests, when upholding it for its own sake should be the major incentive for those who appoint themselves as its spokesmen.

2. The second stance is that of the neo-orthodoxy (*assalafīyya al-jadida*) and the thinkers who are aware of the necessity of overstepping the traditional limits. They do not deny the legislative dimension in the Qur'ān, but they believe that the adjudications and legislations mentioned in it concerning administration (*mu*ᶜ*āmalāt*) may develop as the circumstances surrounding their formulation change. This conciliatory position, supported by most of the figures of the reformation since Mohammed ᶜAbduh, including al Ḥaddād, Ibn Bādīs, and ᶜAllāl al Fāsī, represented undeniable progress in comparison with the traditionalists' views, and required some daring a century ago. However, it could not offer a radical solution because it had no solid theoretical base. Thus, the number of its adherents diminished and it was marginalized by the fundamentalist current.

3. The stance of today's Islamicist movements is based on the belief that any separation between the text and reality is

unacceptable. It is imperative that we change reality by returning to the era of the *as-Salaf as-ṣāliḥ* (the exemplary predecessors) and do not try to re-establish the unity by subjecting the text to reality. This stance is characterized mainly by utopianism and ahistoricity, although it may have a compelling internal logic of its own. That is why it has attracted the young, the troubled and pulverized groups, and the victims of inadequate modernization. Nevertheless, it has always lacked qualified theoreticians, and its leading figures were mostly propagandists rather than scholars.

4. Maḥmūd Mohammed Tāha alone adopted a very bold stand in his book *Ar-risāla al thāniya fī al-Islam,*[56] and he paid for it with his life. He believed that the Mohammedan mission was both a general address to all people in the Meccan era and a specific address to the prophet's contemporaries during the phase of the Medina. In his view we must eliminate from the specific address all those juridical prescriptions that were fit for the conditions of life at the beginning of the fourth century but are no longer so in the second half of the twentieth. It is imperative that we go back to the general address which remains unaltered, no matter how much the circumstances change.[57]

Each of these stances has its own justification and may be valid, depending on the perspective from which it is approached. However, all are dominated by a direct utilitarian objective and the urgent need to find a way out of the culturally debilitated and backward status of Muslims at the present time. Thus, they all confront the issues without a suitable theoretical apparatus and without a dynamic element in their view of history. The deficiency of the tradi-

[56] This book was first published in 1976 in Sūdān, with no mention of the place of publication. Later, a succession of other editions appeared with no mention of dates.

[57] I have analyzed these stances in my book: Abdelmajid Sharfi, *al-Islam wal Ḥadātha* (Islam and Modernity), Tunisia, 1990.

tionalist stance is obvious because it fails to offer a harmonious solution, and the utopian Islamicist stance, being utopian, has no chance of success. Far from deserving the accusations of Islamic societies being behind the times, Islamicism is moving towards new complications, rather than the simplicity that marked the first Islamic community, and towards establishing the values of enlightenment, rather than denying them. Despite the many differences in their views, both Maḥmūd Tāha and the reformists agree on the necessity of reaffirming some parts of the Mohammedan mission and of omitting or reinterpreting others. Nevertheless, nothing can actually guarantee that one interpretation is more valid than another, which is incompatible with it or opposed to it.

Chapter Four

THE ISSUE OF LEGISLATION (TASHRI^{c})

If the situation is correctly summed up at the close of the previous chapter, and we have every reason to believe that it is, we must seek a radical solution that will go beyond spurious compromises, reconcile the contemporary Muslim with his religion, and rid him of the dualism that impedes creativity, hampers initiative, and thwarts the spirit of adventure. That is the reason for our interest in the legislative aspect of the Qur'ān, which has been subject to more arguments and disputes than any other. The first point worthy of note in this context is that the revelation (waḥī) speaks of *shari^{c}a* not in the sense of a sacred law, but rather in the sense of a direction or a course of action (*tarīqa*).[58] The Qur'ān's task is to delineate the course of action that the believer (*Mu'min*) should follow,[59] and in that sense it is binding. However, within this general course of action only a few details of conduct and behavior are indicated and these are usually circumstantial solutions to problems that faced the Muslim community. It is the circumstantial nature of these solutions that explains the discrepancies between them. For the most part the revelation failed to spell out the details in the text (*tanṣīṣ*), whether they related to

[58] "We have made you follow a course in the affair, therefore follow it" (The Kneeling (al-Jathiyah) 45/18).

[59] This is what Mohammad al Tālibī calls the "directed arrow" (al sahm al mūwajah), see Mohammad al Tālibī, *^{c}Iyāl Allah*, Tunis, 1992.

various aspects of life at the time or to whatever might arise later.

Although they primarily pertain to acts of worship, these directives, which are of a moral and educational nature, already existed in the Meccan period and could not be separated from the other major contemporary concerns of the revelation, such as monotheism, the resurrection, judgement day, and the prophetic missions. The command to establish regular prayers, to be charitable and pay the zakāt (alms tax), to do good, to enjoin truthfulness, patience and compassion on each other, to be righteous, pious, and thankful, to honor covenants, to guard one's private parts, to set slaves free, to feed orphans, prisoners, and the poor, to grant blood-relatives and wayfarers their rights–no less than the prohibition of murder, injustice, disobedience, tyranny, pride, obscenity, lechery and adultery, lying and scandal-mongering, backbiting and slander, profligacy and meanness, oppressing the orphan and chiding him who asks–were all concerns of the revelation. They were all signs directing Muslims to the right path, and in no way differ from the precepts about fasting, the *Kiblah* (the direction of the *Kaᶜaba* towards which Muslims turn in prayer), the *Jihād* (Holy war in God's cause), marriage, divorce, theft, and other aspects of the revelation in the Madinese period.

In my view it is as unacceptable to divide the mission into a Meccan and a Madinese one in the manner advocated by Maḥmūd Tahā as it is to break up what is wrongly called 'ayāt al aḥkām' (regulative verses) and to quote these verses out of their historical context and apart from the Qur'ānic text, as jurists have done and are still doing. For Aḥkām is a jurisprudential term that signifies–in descending order–duty, delegation, the licit, the abhorred, and the illicit. These distinctions have no foundation in the prophetic mission, which was concerned with the good and the bad in its own time, and which could therefore only point towards general standards of honorable conduct and moral virtue. What this meant in practice for later generations of Muslims had to be inferred by them on their own. However, in order to be correct, these inferences must not depend on clinging to the letter of the mission and worshiping the text as such, but rather on seeking the spirit of the text with all its meanings and purposes, so that the object of worship would be God alone, and the Muslim's conscience the only judge of his response to the divine instruction.

There is no doubt that this method of reading and understanding can preserve the credibility of the Islamic mission through the different circumstances that may befall Muslims. As far as the Qur'ān's references to Adam and Eve, to Satan, the jinn, demons, angels, and prophetic miracles are concerned, it does no harm for the believer to see all these as symbols and parables deriving from the mythical mentality, and not as historical truth. Nor does it do any harm to consider the prescribed details of worship and administration (ᶜibadāt, muᶜamalāt)—which in any case are very few in number—merely as effects of the communal requirements in the age of the prophet and particularly in the Ḥijāz environment, with its simple relationships and primitive ways of life, which differed greatly from other environments and in particular from those of the modern age everywhere in the world.

If we disregard the large body of work in jurisprudence that exhausted the efforts of generation after generation of scholars, and go back to the Qur'ān's incessant urging to pray, we notice that the text deliberately avoids spelling out the number and form of prayers and their methods. There is no mention of anniyya (the intention to pray), purification and ablution (wudu'), 'Iqāma, Takbīr, the recital of the Fātiḥa and the the sūra or verse (āya) or group of verses, kneeling and prostration, the final greeting (taḥiyya), the difference in the number of rikᶜat from one prayer to another, or the difference between the performance of the Imam (the leader in prayer) and that of the Ma'mun (the follower in prayer) in the event of a collective prayer.[60] It is also evident that the related accounts of the circumstances that determine the ascension prayers (*Miᶜrāj*), and those of the famous bargain between God and the prophet which led, as a result of the intervention of Moses, to the reduction of the number of prayers from fifty to five per day, all belong to the mythological (*Usttōrī*) mentality and are not trustworthy. The prophet prayed in a certain way and the Muslims followed his example,[61] but this does not mean that all Muslims in all times, places, and circumstances are obliged to adhere to that specific mode of prayer, assuming that it was actually unified and did not undergo any alteration during the time of the mission. For, if this were true, the inhabitants of the northern parts of the earth, where the days in summer are so long that night hardly ever falls, and the days in winter are so short that it is almost always night, would not be affected by Mohammed's mission in the same way as the inhabitants of the moderate regions, where the length of the day does not differ much in winter and summer; and the same would apply to the members of industrial communities dominated by the requirements of the machine, as opposed to those in

[60] The only case in which there is some mention of the details of prayer is that of the prayer of fear in the Chapter of Women (4/101–102), notwithstanding Abu Ḥanīfa's view that Muslims were not obliged to pray and could postpone their prayer if they were engaged in battle or if they were in great fear.

[61] However, Al-Rāzī records disagreement among the prophet's companions about the things they supposedly saw him do more than once: "For the companions despite their great care for their religion and their eagerness to regulate it, failed to concur in respect of things they witnessed five times every day, such as whether the prayers were performed singly or in pairs, read aloud, and with hands raised." Fakhredddin al-Razi, *al-Maḥsūl,* 2nd ed., Beirut, Mu'assasat al-Risālah, 1992, vol. 1, p. 214. "Praying in singles or in pairs, being one of the most obvious and self-evident things, was not reported in *tawātur* (i.e. by numerous authorities in agreement). Secondly, the different circumstances of prayer, such as raising the hands or reading aloud, are also among the self-evident issues which were not reported in the same manner," *ibid*, vol. 4, p. 293.

pastoral, agricultural or trading communities. In other words, Mohammed's mission would no longer concern all those whose complicated life styles differ from the simple styles of traditional life.[62]

The forms of worship historians are able to trace back to the time of the revelation and before it—such as ablution (*wudu'*), which the Jews knew in one form or another, the ritual of prayer, as practiced in the Syrian Nestorian Church, and kneeling and prostration (*rukuᶜ and sujūd*)[63]—in no way undermine the authority of the Divine command or the believer's need from time to time to withdraw, contemplate, introspect, and enter into a pious and submissive state, in which he can re-evaluate his deeds and leave worldly concerns behind. This does not mean that I am denying the value of the five daily prayers, the Friday prayer, the prayers of the two feasts, the funeral prayers, or any others. Prayer remains the model of behavior for two types of Muslims: those who believe in its necessity according to the cultural sunna (prescribed way of life) and those whose circumstances allow for a merely conventional performance of it. Nevertheless, there are other types of people who have abandoned prayer or who face a dilemma between reality and a desired ideal way of life. Do these not have the right to be loyal to the imperatives of their religion without having to adhere to all the details decreed by their predecessors?

The situation is similar with regard to the zahāt (alms tax). The Qur'ān does not specify the amount, nor does it indicate

[62] A brief glance at the jurisprudential encyclopedias of all schools suffices to make one recognize the difference between the vast amount of detail they contain, in contrast to the Qur'ān's mere prompting to prayer. However, these details only relate to societies of one type, which had either already ceased to exist or was very near its end with respect to its modes of life and methods of production.

[63] The classical work about this subject, albeit from an initially Christian perspective, is Friedrich Heiler's book, translated into English under the title: *Prayer, A Study in the History and Psychology of Religion*, Oxford University Press, 1932.

what it has to be paid for. Nevertheless, the concept remains valid at an absolute level and shows the need for solidarity between the rich and the poor. In contrast, insisting on the types of money that existed at the time of the prophet, and on similar ways of spending it, only reveals a narrow perspective and ignorance of its real purpose. Such an attitude also shows an unawareness of the modern ways of cooperation, which represent a great step forward in comparison to the ancient forms of charity and benevolence, and which are probably closer to the spirit of the mission in considering the poor as having a right to the wealth of the rich.[64] These modern forms of charity have greater resources and more highly developed ways of collecting and spending them. They preserve the dignity of the needy and provide them with services that were neglected in past civilizations, but have by now become human rights, such as the right to education, work, a home, health care, and others things.

I demonstrated in an earlier work[65] that the Qur'ān prompts Muslims in various ways to fast—"fasting is prescribed to you as it was prescribed to those before you" (The Cow 2/183), "that you fast is better for you" (2/184), "whoever of you is present in the month, he shall fast therein" (2/185)—but leaves the door open for the possibility of not fasting and compensating for this by feeding the poor. The ayāt relating to this—in particular "those who are able to do it may effect a redemption by feeding a poor man" and "Allah desires ease for you and He does not desire difficulty for you" (2/184-185)—were not interpreted as rejecting the possibility of compensation for fasting through charity until

[64] Doctor Maḥmūd Sudqī was the first to raise the issue of prayer and the poor-rate (*zakāt*) in the modern age. See his article "Al Islam hūwa Al Quran Waḥdahu" (Islam is the Quran alone), *Al Manar*, 1906, issue 9, pp. 515-525.

[65] On verses 283-187 in the chapter of The Cow, published in the volume *Buhuth Muhdāt ila Muhammad al-Tālibī* (Researches dedicated to Muhammad al-Tālibī), Tunis, 1993, and republished in *Labanat*.

after the prophet's death, whereas it was accepted in his lifetime. Modern Muslims avoid a direct confrontation with the Qur'ānic text, which they still read through the apparatuses of the old jurists and interpreters. That is why it is no surprise to see many of them fall into one of two predicaments: either submitting to social conventions without any conviction and pretending to fast—and this is surely not the purpose for which this act of worship was decreed—or resorting to jurisprudential ploys such as arguing that the inhabitants of the regions to the north or south of a certain latitude (45 degrees) must fast according to the timing of that latitude without regard to the sunset or sunrise.[66]

It is also known that the *ḥajj*, or pilgrimage to Mecca, was a ritual practiced by the Arabs before the rise of Islam. Islam adopted it and ascribed to it a new significance in accordance with monotheism. Nevertheless, one cannot deny the traces of the ancient mythical mentality which remain evident in the rites of pilgrimage, including stoning the devils (*rajm*) and the slaughter of the sacrificial animal (*hadi*). I do not wish to deny either the release of repressed urges or the positive channeling of violence provided by the act of stoning: both are constant human needs. But why should a Muslim who has an aversion to stoning be compelled to do it? Does a Muslim not have a right to favor self-determination over conforming to something of which he is not fully convinced?

I did not intend to raise issues related to the pillars of Islam (arkān al Islam) or its laws (shara'i[c]) for the mere purpose of opposing certain religious sentiments, and I have

[66] M. Hamidullah, "Le musulman dans le milieu occidental" (Muslims in the Western World), in *Normes et valeurs dans l'islam contemporain* (*Norms and Values in Contemporary Islam*), Paris, Payot, 1996, pp. 200–205. There are millions of Muslims living in these regions, particularly in northern Europe and America. They are mostly immigrants, although some of the natives of these regions have also embraced Islam, and by far outnumber the Muslim contemporaries of the prophet.

emphasized that whoever is convinced of the necessity of adhering to the ways of worship decreed by the jurists should follow them. Neither I nor anybody else is entitled to disparage the subjective personal emotion that accompanies the different methods of worship in any religion. Moreover, I do not believe that these methods can easily be changed or developed through any individual or collective decision, nor am I certain whether or not this change is generally desired. It is true that these "pillars," whether jointly or separately, have been increasingly abandoned in everyday reality, due not to an essential denial of them but rather to the vast changes in the circumstances of life since the times of our fathers and grandfathers. However, pointing out the problem and seeking a satisfactory solution to it do not mean creating that problem or sailing in troubled waters. Al Ghazāli in *Iḥyā' ^cUlūm al Dīn* repeats the phrase "Consult your heart"—a rule fit for Muslims to follow in order to bridge the gap between religion and life and to quit a blind conformity based on no reasonable evidence or proof. There is no doubt that abstinence from lying is a religious demand and a condition for psychological stability, and whoever does not lie must be able to express himself without being harmed or ostracized. This can never be, unless freedom is revered as a condition incapable of any compromise.

If the situation regarding the acts of worship (*^cibadāt*) were as portrayed, then those commands and prohibitions mentioned in the Qur'ān that were called for by the circumstances of the Islamic community at the time of the mission would pose a less severe problem. However, a solution can only be found on the basis of considering the Qur'ān as an integral whole, where separating some of its verses (*ayāt*) from the rest is inconceivable, and where the purpose aimed at in each situation must be borne in mind. Moreover, the solution depends on an awareness of the causes that led Muslims in the past to interpret the Qur'ān in certain ways and to restrict their meditation and speculation (*tadabur*) to less than one-tenth of its more than six thousand *ayāt*, without paying any regard to the repetitions since many of those *ayāt* are purely informative (Ikhbāri) and have no stylistic quality (Inshā'ī).[67] In any case, the material contained in the Qur'ān only represents a small part of the *Aḥkām* (regulations) the jurists set down and thought they had inferred with absolute certainty. The necessity of giving consideration to the changing circumstances surrounding these regulations is beyond doubt, for instance in relation to details of conduct and to punishments for transgressions as practiced by the Jews, and the prohibition on icons, which was needed at a time when idol-worship was not yet far away, but which is no longer valid in a civilization relying on the image in its various forms, as found in the cinema, television, newspapers, magazines, etc.

The Qur'ān does not decree the abolition of slavery, although it encourages the liberating of slaves and allows many occasions for the abolition of this phenomenon, which is incompatible with human dignity. However, the issue of slavery is no longer an issue in our own times. There are many other unsettled issues that require an urgent solution because they trouble the religious conscience and result in many concessions, antagonisms, and miseries that may end in the shedding of blood and the sacrifice of many innocent souls. These issues include apostasy (ar-ridda), capital punishment, theft, usury (ar-ribā), and the relationship between religion and the management of the state and the family.

I begin with apostasy because the Qur'ān contains no mention, either direct or indirect, of any earthly punishment for an apostate, but rather stipulates a punishment in the afterlife, which is not for any human being to carry out. Nevertheless, the amazing thing is that many Muslims, including some who are considered scholars, believe the punishment of an apostate to be one of the religious decrees, based on a

[67] It is enough in this respect to review the interpretations that deal exclusively with *'Ayāt al-Aḥkām'*, such as *Aḥkām al-* Qur'ān by Al Jaṣṣaṣ, Al Kayyā al Harāsī, and Ibn Arabī, and *Jāmiᶜ Aḥkām al-* Qur'ān by Al Qurṭobī.

weak ḥadīth (daᶜīf)—the prophet's saying "Kill him who changes his religion"—and on the way Abū Bakr dealt with the apostates (ahl ar-ridda). What is also surprising is the ascendancy of the communal dictates of the old systems over the essential concept of religious freedom which was promulgated by the Mohammedan mission and which tolerates no exceptions or hesitations.[68] It is feared that if an apostate were not threatened by the penalty (ḥadd) of death, the weak-hearted—deluded into believing that he had left Islam after experiencing it and discovering it to be wanting—would follow his example, and thus the number of Muslims would decrease. This assumes that morality lies in the literal significance of deeds and not in conviction and voluntary faith, but is not restricted to this particular issue, since every prophetic mission in due course becomes subject to an exegesis that causes it to deviate from its aims under the yoke of socio-historical coercions. In fact, the exegesis itself may ultimately contradict the mission precisely where it believes itself to be faithful to it.[69]

As for capital punishment, it is quite clear that killing a human being is a crime deserving punishment, according to all laws, regardless of their source. Although the Qur'ān states that the punishment of a murderer is death, it confines this punishment to the killer himself, excluding any of his

[68] See Amāl al-Qarāmī, *Qadiyyat al-Ridda fi al-Fikr Al-Islami* (The Issue of Apostasy in Islamic Thought), DRA in the Faculty of Arts at Manouba, 1993. The central thesis of Mohammad Charfi's book, *Islam et liberté* (Islam and Liberty), Paris, 1999, is the essential incongruity of jurisprudence and the concept of liberty on the issue of apostasy as on many other issues.

[69] Although this deviation is a widespread phenomenon that manifests itself in various ways, we may cite, as one example, the following sentence from the Tunisian newspaper *Al Sabāḥ* of 20/2/1994: "And probably one of the most essential rules for establishing civilized conduct is to follow the Almighty's saying: 'If ye disobey, conceal yourselves'." Neither the editors nor the readers of the newspaper rejected this false attribution of hypocrisy to God.

relatives who were previously thought to deserve that punishment as well. Moreover, the Qur'ān leaves the possibility of pardon and forgiveness open if the family of the victim agrees to it. This recognizes the principle of personal—rather than collective—punishment, and it also goes beyond a mere mechanical execution of the punishment, contrary to what the jurists came to decree later on. The way the Qur'ān handles the issue of capital punishment indicates that the purpose of the penalty lies not in the penalty itself but rather in the way the penalty responds to the simple requirements of the community. Therefore, the substitution of prison or any other form of penalty for capital punishment would not conflict with the general Qur'ānic principle. Today the state alone has the right to legalized violence and the responsibility for disciplining all types of criminals. In earlier days, under the aegis of the tribal system and in the absence of state institutions, it was the right of the victim's guardian to take revenge. In view of this progress, nothing stands in the way of taking a further step towards eliminating capital punishment altogether, especially since the complex systems of modern metropolitan life cannot absolutely guard the sentences passed by judges from error, in which case the innocent would be the victims. Preserving the life of a person accused of a crime would increase the possibility of rectifying a wrong judgment, while killing the person would make it impossible. I do not believe that the Muslim conscience would allow one innocent life to fall victim to the strict adherence to methods of punishment that were justified in the old simple communities but are no longer so in our own day.

There are Muslims who believe that cutting off a thief's hand is one of the divine commands that do not tolerate exegesis, because it seems to be stated in absolute terms in a holy text.[70] I have written elsewhere[71] about the long-

[70] "And the man who steals and the woman who steals, cut off their hands as a punishment for what they have earned, an exemplary punishment from Allah, and Allah is mighty and wise" (al Ma'idah, 5/38).

standing arguments of the interpreters and the jurists over the meaning of "cutting off" and "hand," as well as the extent of the cut. They have decreed that theft is only the taking of forbidden money or money in which the thief has no just share, as with public money, and many of them have resorted to different ploys in order to avoid the execution of this penalty. That is the position of Sunni Islamic thought in general, which maintains the ideal at the theoretical level, but tolerates any number of solutions that may deviate from it at the practical level, such as avoiding the penalty for the sake of the positive law or of the collective conscience, which is appalled by such a penalty. Dealing with the issue from a socio-historical perspective can spare Muslims this troubling dualism.

There is no doubt that cutting off the thief's hand was a practice known before the rise of Islam and it is only natural that the penalty for theft was so severe in the context of the tribal community and a subsistence economy in general, in which a person whose money was stolen could be totally ruined. Such a severe penalty may have been the only means of maintaining a minimum standard of order in the absence of a political authority whose power would have prevailed over all members of the society concerned. Moreover, corporal punishment in general—beating, whipping, amputation and even execution—was thought normal and indispensable for the evolution of society and the maintenance of its stability. Thus, what the Qur'ān decreed was in complete agreement with the requirements of the time. However, this does not rule out the possibility of other forms of punishment once the societies have developed and acquired values that make all forms of torture and corporal punishment appear

[71] ^cAbdelmajid Sharfi, *Taḥdith al Fikr al-Islamī* (Modernizing Islamic Thought), Casablanca, 1998, pp. 49–51. See also Na'īla Slīnī, *Tarīkhīyyat al Tafsīr al Quranī wa al ^cAlāqāt al Ijtima^cīyya* (The Historicity of Qur'ānic Interpretation and Social Relationships), a PhD thesis prepared for the Faculty of Arts at Manouba, 1998, pp. 166–193.

incompatible with the principle of human dignity. In other words, cutting off the thief's hand, like any other penalty, is not an end in itself and there is no harm in abandoning it for other forms of punishment more in tune with the circumstances of modern Islamic societies, as long as the purpose of the punishment as such is fulfilled. The abolition of this penalty in most Muslim countries has certainly not distanced Muslims from the spirit of Mohammed's mission and the execution of it in the very few countries which still adhere to it—with reference to Islamic law (*shariʿa*)—appalls rational Muslims even more than many others. This is what Mohammad Iqbal stated more than seventy years ago: "The primary source of the Law of Islam is the Qur'ān. The Qur'ān, however, is not a legal code. Its main purpose is to awaken in man the higher consciousness of his relation with God and the universe." And he adds: "The prophet's method is to train one particular people, and to use them as a nucleus for the building up of a universal Shari'a. In doing so he accentuates the principles underlying the social life of all mankind, and applies them to concrete cases in the light of the specific habit of the people immediately before him. The Shariʿat values (aḥkām) resulting from this application (e.g. rules relating to the penalties of crimes) are in a sense specific to that people; and, *since their observance is not an end in itself, they cannot be strictly enforced in the case of future generations.*"[72]

The issue of usury seems to be approaching its solution. The fundamental question here is whether or not lending or borrowing money with interest through banks or other similar institutions is considered usury. In this context, two facts are worth recalling. The first is that the prohibition of usury exists in both Judaism and Christianity and none of the followers of these two religions nowadays consider it

[72] Mohammad Iqbāl, *The Reconstruction of Religious Thought in Islam*, Lahore, 1958, pp. 165–172 (italics mine).

applicable to lending with interest. The second is that the prohibition of usury, confirmed in more than one verse of the Qur'ān, is the prohibition of a specific type of loan where the interest is "doubly doubled." It is a transaction between two parties which enriches one effortlessly and at the expense of the other, who happens to be in need of money at a certain time. Moreover, failure to pay that excessively high interest may even lead to the enslavement of the debtor. Thus, the Qur'ān's prohibition of usury (ribā) is justified and uniformly valid in all cases of such extreme and unlawful exploitation.

Obtaining loans subject to interest from a bank is not subject to interdiction. Firstly, it is not a transaction between two individuals but between an individual human being on the one hand and a banking firm on the other. Banks did not exist at the time of the prophet, so how could something that did not exist in reality be forbidden? Secondly, the interest charged for a a loan by a bank is not usury, because it is the state that determines it in advance, taking account of inflation, the costs of financial transactions, the taxes imposed on the bank, the revenues from the money lent, and many other circumstances. Rather than having the consequences of usury (ribā), this stimulates economic life and encourages productive enterprises. It clearly avoids the injustices done to those who are obliged to take loans from usurers in some Islamic countries and others—like India—in the absence of institutions governing people's rights and duties. Thus I may return to the general theoretical principle established earlier, which requires us to look into the motivation of the Qur'ānic commands and prohibitions, and the moral purpose or message behind them. This, in my view, is by far preferable to the ploys and different forms of jugglery to which "Islamic banks" resort on the recommendation of some official religious organizations. The truth is that the relationship between these "Islamic banks" and Islam is only nominal. In fact, the interest these "Islamic banks" charge under various misleading labels in the name of Islam may well be higher than normal bank interest and benefit the parties that control them rather than their deluded clients.[73]

If banking has become a normal phenomenon in several Islamic countries, it is because it falls under the many economic transactions which are subject to positive law and because the Islamic conscience no longer finds fault with secularized transactions. The situation is different with respect to the institutions of the state and the family, which, in modern societies, are the two institutions that resist secularization more than any others. Moreover, the religious argument concerning these two institutions is very hard to challenge, let alone overcome, because it has been confirmed for centuries from generation to generation. In fact, the derivation of the ruler's power from a divine right, in the conventional religious understanding, is the guarantee for the stability and for the submissive acceptance of that power. What else would justify the ruler's entitlement to practice legalized violence in directing the society and arbitrating in the disputes that inevitably arise between its members? This was the most suitable solution for both the ruler and the ruled and did not encounter any objection until the rise of the nation state from the ruins of the old empires, when the state acquired definite boundaries and all its citizens became subject to the same law.

Those who hold an essentialist view of religion often overlook this important historical element. They ascribe the separation between religion and the state in modern western

[73] On the subject of bank interests and usury, see Abdullah Saeed, *Islamic Banking and Interest. A Study of the Prohibition of Ribā and its Contemporary Interpretation*, Leiden, 1996. This study confirms what I had already deduced in my book *Islam et liberté* (Islam and Liberty) about the ploys to which these banks resort and which they claim to be in accordance with the shariʿa, whereas in fact they merely change the names of their transactions. In that context I also recorded the daring stand taken by the Shaykh of al-Azhar in 1998, when he spoke out in favour ordinary banks over the so-called "Islamic banks."

societies to the nature of Christianity.[74] In their view, Christianity is a religion that gives "unto Caesar the things that are Caesar's" and "unto God the things that are God's," and its founder, Jesus, did not pursue any worldly power, unlike Islam, in which the prophet always combined spiritual and temporal authority. Thus, they conclude that Islam by its nature calls for the union of religion and the state. In this they not only overlook the struggles that took place in Christian countries and ended in the exclusion of the clergy from the political sphere, but they also disregard the nature of the power practiced by the Muslim ruler and its relation to religious people history. A detailed description of the actual practice of leadership over the epochs and in the different Muslim states is provided by Ibn Khaldūn's analysis of leadership in all its forms.

However, what interests me at this point is the relationship between the Mohammedan mission and Mohammed's behavior from the time he left Mecca and migrated to the Madina till his death. In that period, which extended over ten years, the prophet himself led a number of conquests and sent his companions on others. He was the unrivaled leader of the nucleus which would later become the vast Islamic Empire, and the final arbitrator in the disputes that emerged between Muslims about a variety of matters. Each one of the three phenomena–the prophet's use of violence, his leadership of the Muslim community, and his arbitration between disputants–requires a justification of his stance and its significance at that particular time.

Was it Mohammed who initiated the use of violence every time? Did not the Quraysh force him to resort to violence because he had to protect the Islamic community, which was still in its infancy? The Quraysh saw the new religion as a

[74] In fact, this separation is not maintained in all cases, even if the rules of democracy generally restrict the use of religion to serve the state. US President George Bush's widely published address to the troops sent to the Arabian Gulf in August 1990 may serve as an example.

threat to their trade interests and as the eradication of the foundations of the system that served these interests. Consequently, they resorted first to a variety of appeals and then to oppression. Thus, it became inevitable that Mohammed would destroy the Quraysh tribal solidarity (ᶜassabīyya), which also comprised the tribes surrounding them, and make their leaders realize—by force when all persuasion proved vain—the uselessness of resistance. It is probable that only the raid on Tabū́k near the border of the Byzantine Empire can be considered an offensive military attack. But even this raid, which resulted in the spread of Islam beyond Ḥijāz and the Arab Peninsula, proved bloodless, and its main purpose was to test the firmness of the Muslims' faith and the strength of their lines—which included the Bedouins who lived around the Madina and who had newly turned Muslim—as compared to the irresolute, whom the Qur'ān calls the "hypo-crites" (*almunāfiqūn*); especially since it occurred in the period of heat and during the incident of Dhirar's Mosque (*masjid Dhirar*), which seems to have been built as a rival to the prophet's mosque (*masjid al rasūl*). In any case, all the indications are showing that the motive of this raid was neither to obtain booty nor to divert attention towards an outside enemy, as would happen later during the Muslim conquests in the reign of the first two Rashidun Caliphs.[75]

Some may find this kind of *realpolitik* blameworthy, just as some may consider the way the Jews were dealt with cruel, but the religious mission was obliged to consider the laws of human society if it was to enter history. These laws take the actual balance of forces into account and do not tolerate any internal or external opposition. Those who reject this realism must be asked whether the spread of any of the monotheistic religions came about without the use of

[75] al-Tabari's interpretation of the Chapter of the Immunity (al-Tawba, al Barā'ah) in his *Tafsīr* contains many elements that reveal the real issues involved in this raid, which were obscured by considerations related to alliances after the time of the mission.

violence, or whether the Mohammedan mission could have had any chance of drawing Arabs and non-Arabs together, had it remained restricted to a few hundred oppressed Muslims, whom the Quraysh threatened and planned to exterminate by all possible means, and in whom the Jews implanted doubt and skepticism in an attempt to defend the Jewish religion, which they feared would be marginalized or fused into the emerging new community. Violence, therefore, was not so much a requirement of Islam as something imposed on it by circumstances. Moreover, any attempt at interpreting the verses concerning war in isolation from the historical context is an unacceptable distortion of the historical truth.[76]

As for the prophet's leadership of the Muslim community in Medina, many Muslims believe that this must be viewed in the context of what they call "the Prophet's State." The truth of the matter is that Mohammed did not assume any of the titles–such as king or prince–that would have indicated his leadership of that alleged state to both Arabs and non-Arabs at the time. Furthermore, while any state requires a minimum level of institutions, the prophet had neither his own currency nor any councils, officials or permanent employees. All he did was to assign some individuals to perform certain occasional tasks such as the administration of justice in some regions, or the command of one of the invasions or conquests. For the rest, his moral authority was enough to unite the Muslims around him. The main difference between him and the heads of tribes was probably that their power was confined to their tribes, while his power transcended tribal allegiances without negating them. In addition, their authority derived from their standing in relation to the

[76] See Adbelmajid Sharfi, "Al-Islam wal ᶜUnf" (Islam and Violence), *Labanat,* pp. 183–190. Although I agree with the analysis presented in that chapter, I have not considered the influence of the conquests in the times of ᶜUmar and ᶜUthmān in particular on the prevalent exegesis, which ultimately justifies aggressive violence by claiming that those conquests were jihād (Holy war) similar to that conducted by the prophet himself.

members of their tribe and from certain traits, such as chivalry, generosity, and prowess, required by their position as leader, while Mohammed's authority rested on a religious basis, which they lacked. This is why his authority could not be delegated or set as an example, but had to end with his death and with the delivery of his mission.[77]

The debate over whether the prophet's role in the Madinese period was that of religious or a political leader, as delineated by ᶜAli ᶜAbdul Rāziq in his renowned book *Islam and the Origins of Rule*, should have ended with Ataturk's elimination of the Caliphate and his introduction of a new ruling system, which did not have the slightest effect on the Muslims' religious practices. This would have been possible, but for the great impact of tradition and the difficulty of transition from the framework of a traditional Empire, which depends on religion to acquire legitimacy, to the framework of a modern nation state, founded on the principle of the free general election of its officials, the sovereignty of the public will manifested in the laws enacted by parliaments, the separation of the executive, legislative, and judicial powers, and the equality of all citizens with respect to their rights and obligations, regardless of their sex, religion, or any other considerations.

We must still study the moral rules generated by the Qur'ān during the Madinese period, and the sayings and deeds ascribed to the prophet and considered to be divine mandatory laws in the jurisprudential system created by the scholars of the second century after the Hegira. Needless to say, the prophet performed, in relation to the emigrants (al-muhājirūn) and the supporters (al-ansār), a daily educating role in changing any elements in their mentalities and behavior that conflicted with Islamic values, which reject tribal bravery and which advocate mercy, harmony and doing

[77] It is worth pointing out here that the Qur'ān distinguishes Solomon from the other prophets by making him ask for a kingdom that is "not fit for anyone" after him (Chapter of Ṣād 38/35).

good. Mohammed continued to present a model of uprightness and virtue without disregarding human nature and the moods and dispositions of his companions, which may have been characterized by gentleness or harshness, jealousy or magnanimity, resoluteness or hesitancy, love of this world or spirituality, etc. In general Mohammed, according to the Qur'ānic expression, was a "good example" (ᶜUswaḥasana).[78] In all the things he indicated, commanded and prohibited, the eschatological horizon was constantly present. The significance and weight of people's deeds and inner thoughts were determined exclusively with reference to that horizon. In other words, the prophet did not pay as much attention to the rules of social organization as he did to those aspects of society that might be in agreement or in conflict with his mission of mercy, human dignity, and preparation for the final judgment. That is why he sanctioned those existing customs which did not clash with the principles of his mission on the one hand, and firmly insisted on the individual's responsibility for both the good and the bad that results from human actions on the other. Therefore, it is not possible to consider the directives of the revelation (waḥī) as the abolition of individual responsibility, revoked by the requirements of the Islamic communion after the prophet's death. Moreover, we cannot pretend to forget what the revelation restates time and again, that Mohammed resembled the prophets before him in that he created, as they had, a book in order that "men might stand by justice" (57/25). He is only a reminder, a herald, a witness, and a harbinger, not the people's master or guardian, and he only directs, but cannot coerce them, into faith: "Every soul is pledged for what it earns" (The Covered (*al-Muddathir*) 74/38), "nor shall one

[78] It is worth noting that this expression is also applied to Abraham in the context of the call for monotheism: "Ye had a good example in Abraham and those with him when they said unto their people, 'Verily we are clear of you and of what ye serve beside God'" (The Tried 60/4), and in verse 6 of the same *sūra*.

bearing a burden bear the burden of another" (The Cattle (*al 'Ann^c^am*) 7/164).[79]

In the light of these unalterable facts we can understand the Qur'ānic call for obedience to the prophet coupled with obedience to God and the revelation's demand for a fair division of wealth, so that "it may not be a thing taken by turn among the rich," and its directive "What the Apostle gives you, take; and what he forbids you, desist from" (The Banishment (*al-Ḥashr*) 59/7). In all the problems faced by Mohammed as he supervised the emerging Islamic nation—whether these related to simple rules of conduct, such as greeting, asking permission, and entering houses, to buying, selling, mortgaging, and lending, to dealing with recipients of earlier revelations (*ahl al kitāb*), unbelievers, and hypocrites, or to marriage, divorce, adultery, and inheritance—the constant characteristics of the revelation or the deeds of the prophet were realism and consideration of the circumstances of life at that time on the one hand, and guidance of the different aspects of human behavior towards the best possible way on the other. The prophet achieved this without using force or coercion, for he neither compelled anyone to do anything without conviction nor used the threat of any worldly consequences, in the manner of others who appoint themselves guardians of religion and make the apparent uniformity of collective conduct an aim against which sincerity and fidelity fade away.

But does this not conflict with the role the Qur'ān assigns to the prophet as the arbitrator of disputes which may arise between Muslims?[80] No, for in the absence of a centralised

[79] These notions are spread over the whole of the Qur'ān, in both the Meccan and the Madinese sūras. There is no need for any specific references, because they concern the fundamental principles of the mission, and any matters related to specific circumstances must be considered in the light of these principles.

[80] "But no! By thy Lord! They will not believe until they have made thee judge of what they differ on; then they will not find in themselves

state and permanently appointed judges, resorting to an arbitrator to resolve disagreements between individuals was well known to the Arab tribes. The litigants agreed in advance to accept the judgment of the arbitrator approved by both parties. The novelty here is that the prophet became judge by virtue of his religious and moral authority, which transcended that of the arbitrators "whose houses litigants visit," as the Arab saying goes, and which belonged to him alone. In other words, his ruling was regarded as "God's judgment" in every particular incident, with the purpose of nurturing the Muslims on Islamic values and principles based on justice and equality, rather than on those of a system in which the social and economic interests of the strong were pursued at the expense of the poor and weak. Changing values and morals is not an easy thing to do, especially in Bedouin societies or societies close to Bedouinism, which were founded on traditions and customs, and where imitation was the prevalent approach. Nevertheless, it was in order to bring about this change that the prophet was obliged to perform his role as a judge and arbitrator perfectly in all respects, but without getting bogged down in the details of this or that particular incident.

My focus on these aspects necessarily leads to a reversal of the postulates established in Islamic consciousness since the second century after the Hegira and to an acknowledg-

---

aught to hinder what thou hast decreed, and they will submit with submission" (Women (an-Nisā') 3/65). Nevertheless, the prophet was aware of his limited human abilities and he never claimed perfection, whether when expressing his opinions or when arbitrating between disputants. He said: "I am only a human being and litigants with cases of dispute come to me, and someone of you may happen to be more eloquent (in presenting his case) than the other, whereby I may consider that he is truthful and pass a judgment in his favor. If ever I pass a judgment in the favor of somebody whereby he takes a Muslim's right unjustly, then whatever he takes is nothing but a piece of Fire, and it is up to him to take or leave," *Saḥiḥ al Bukhāri*, the book of Judgments, the chapter on being granted the right of one's brother by mistake.

ment of the fact that the purpose lies neither in the specificity of the reasons nor in the generality of the words. We must examine the purpose and intention beyond the specific reasons and the words used to indicate them. This examination will provide scope for exegeses that differ in accordance with the needs of people and their environment, culture, time, etc. It will also provide scope for progress, once we realize that the import of the mission concerns us, here and now, without being bound to the understanding adopted by the prophet's contemporaries–of which we know very little–or by the exegesis succeeding generations of Muslims settled for. It sometimes seems as if today's Muslims, by imitating their scholars and the Imams of their sects and groups, are falling into the same error as the earlier aḥl al kitāb, whom the Qur'ān reprehends for worshiping gods other than God. It seems as if they are unaware of the flexibility that characterizes the mission and marks Mohammed's behavior, which they have reduced to a mere matter of memory rather than meditation and reflection.

The changes that occurred in the course of the mission may be exemplified by a simple comparison between the stand of the prophet, who did not go beyond slapping the drinker of wine with the side of his robe, a palm-leaf stalk, or a shoe, and that of ᶜUmar b. a. Khattāb and ᶜAli b. Abu Tālib, who decreed whipping,[81] and who were followed by most jurists in considering the drinking of wine an offense requiring punishment (*Iqāmat al ḥadd*). Another example is the prophet's treatment of the man who copulated with a woman during Ramadan, in contrast with the references to expiatory

[81] Ali's view in this matter was based on an analogy which is not valid in all cases: when he drinks wine, he becomes drunk and if he becomes drunk he raves and if he raves he slanders, and "the penalty for slander is eighty lashes." But he also says: "When I sentence one to a penalty and he dies, I only feel sorrow in my heart if he were a drinker of wine. If he dies I pay his blood money (*dīyya*) because the prophet did not decree it." Fakhreddin al Rāzī, *al Maḥsūl,* 4/190.

gifts (kaffāra) and the attempt at codifying the minutest details of the abstinence required during the fasting period, with which the books of jurisprudence are replete. The prophet asked the man to do penance by giving alms, but since he was too poor to do so, the prophet collected from the man's friends a sufficient amount for him to give away. However, the man, believing that he was poor enough to receive the alms himself, kept them, with the prophet's consent.[82] One only needs to compare the behavior of the prophet with that of the jurists to recognize the essential difference between his code of conduct, which is characterized by forgiveness, flexibility, and support, and the highly conservative code the jurists tried to impose on Muslims.

Similarly, the mission made sure not to deprive women of their right to inherit, whereas the Imams of the schools and their followers considered the verses that deal with this principle as final and mandatory solutions, even though in many cases—like all the other verses concerning inheritance—they can only be applied arbitrarily in the context of what scholars of al Farā'd call alᶜAul (the excess that remains of the inheritance after the shares (farā'd) are distributed). The issue of polygamy is connected with this. The Qur'ān mentions it once at the beginning of the Chapter of Women in connection with the fear of not being able "to deal justly with the orphans" (Women 4/127). It advocates justice between wives, but asserts in verse 129 of the same chapter that this justice is impossible, although men may wish to achieve it. At the same time it allows taking concubines from

[82] Al-Khattīb al-Baghdadi comments of this incident as follows: "this account contains two judgments: the first is general and decrees the necessity of delivering expiatory gifts (kaffāra) by him who contravenes the demand for abstinence by copulating with his woman in Ramadan, as mentioned above: the second is specific and lies in the prophet's permission for the man to take the collected money, a permission that can only be granted by the prophet and none other than him!" *Al-Faqih w al-Mutafaqih*, second edition, Beirut, 1980, vol. 1, pp. 110–111.

what a man "possesses in his right hand" (*Mulk al yāmīn*) i.e. in his power or under his control. In other words, a free man may have as many legitimate sexual relationships as he wants, and is capable of, with slave women or bondwomen. In fact, the Qur'ān was simply describing certain customs that were widespread among Arabs and in other traditional societies–and some of which, like beating, are no longer acceptable in our times–while directing them towards good behavior and the rejection of injustice and exploitation.

Nevertheless, later Muslims have dealt with women in a manner as far removed from these directives as possible, if not completely in opposition to them. That is why we must today reconsider all the views of the dichotomy of man and woman as one of hierarchy and not just one of difference and complementariness, views of woman as an object of man's pleasure rather than a being who, like man, has rights and obligations, and views that demean woman and limit her freedom by imposing the veil on her, and by restricting her to the home and to her reproductive task. Whether they like it or not, modern Islamic societies in the process of moving from traditional modes of life and production towards industrialism and integration into the present "international order"–like all other societies with different religions and cultures–are undergoing an unmistakable conversion to acknowledging the rights of which women have been deprived throughout history. I do not consider this a denial of the values of the mission, even though it involves casting away a great deal of what the mission had temporarily decreed as a result of its realism, and despite the objections of the social groups that would prefer women to remain inferior and as a result believe themselves to be more eager than others to remain loyal to their religious teachings.[83]

[83] Tunisia is considered a pioneer among Islamic countries in this respect. *Majalat al aḥwāl al shakhsiyya* has completely forbidden polygamy since 1957, assigned the exclusive right to decree divorce to the courts, granted women the right to choose their husbands and to receive their

While I am discussing issues related to the family system, I cannot avoid confronting that of adultery and its penalty. It is well-known that the penalty mentioned in the Qur'ān is 'whipping'[84] and not 'stoning' to death, as decided by the jurists on the basis of a verse, the actual words of which were repealed, and of an unverified precedent referred to by the prophet. Further, the whipping administered for adultery is only slightly more severe than that for libel (*al-Qadhf*) in the specific sense of accusing a person of adultery without producing four witnesses.[85] In the first instance the penalty is a hundred lashes, reduced to half in the case of bond-women or slave girls, and in the second case eighty lashes. The purpose of this penalty was to prevent the spread of obscenities and the mingling of lineages, particularly in a society where the purity of lineage was thought to be of extreme importance. In Bedouin societies, there was no need for men to resort to illegitimate sexual relationships, since they were allowed to marry more than one woman and to take as many concubines from among their slaves as they wished.[86] Moreover, there was also the temporary—or *'al-mutᶜa'*—marriage. Whether this was repealed, as the Sunnis claim, or not, as the Shi'ites have always maintained, it is practiced in Iran to this day and specifically serves the

fathers' inheritance without including blood relatives where there are no sons, etc. Although these daring progressive laws have conflicted with many discriminatory systems that have deprived woman of her simplest rights, such as the right to study or to drive a car, they definitely represent the path to the future.

[84] "As for the fornicatress and the fornicater, flog each of them, (giving) a hundred lashes, and let not pity for them detain you in the matter of obedience to Allah" (The Light (An-Nur) 24/2).

[85] "And those who accuse free women then do not bring four witnesses, flog them (giving) eighty lashes, and do not admit evidence from them ever; and these it is that are the transgressors" (The Light (An-Nur) 24/4).

[86] "If they are guilty of indecency, they shall suffer half the punishment which is inflicted upon free women" (Women (an-Nisā') 4/25).

interests of the men adhering to the religion.[87] The novelty involved in the rules for whipping, which has been inconceivable to Islamic society throughout the ages[88], was the equality between males and females on one hand and the rigorous conditions, such as the presence of four witnesses, imposed on the penalty, which made it practically impossible to execute.

Another case worth considering is the *ᶜidda* (waiting period) of a divorced or widowed woman. The purpose of these waiting periods was to make sure that she was not pregnant from her previous marriage. That is why it was imposed on the woman and not the man, who can remarry without having to wait. But cannot this procedure be replaced, in our modern days, with accurate scientific means of testing pregnancy? Are we supposed to close our eyes to all the new discoveries in the fields of medicine and the life sciences, which were unknown at the time of the revelation, and to content ourselves with the primitive ways, blindly adhering to the letter of texts without even trying to understand the purposes behind them in the light of the progress of science? Those who constantly repeat the motto of "harmony between the intellect and sound tradition" would be well advised to think about this issue, and many others like it, in order to realize that the accounts need to be interpreted in all cases and that the best exegesis is the one that preserves the

[87] On this subject see Shahla Haeri, *Law of Desire. Temporary Marriage in Iran*, London, 1989. Originally a PhD thesis prepared in the United States, this work is concerned with the *mutᶜa* marriage in Iran, the *ᶜUrfi* marriage in Egypt, and the ***Misyyār*** marriage in the Arab Peninsula. It was translated into Arabic by Abdullah Kamal, as *Al Daᶜara Al Hallāl* (The Lawful Prostitution), Beirut, 1997.

[88] The most recent example is the Jordanian parliament's refusal in 1999 to amend the law which permits the killing of an adulteress, but not that of an adulterer, by a member of her tribe or family. It is common knowledge that many women fall victim to this practice as a result of mere accusation, suspicion, or gossip. This practice bears no relation to the Qur'ān or Islam.

spirit of the text, rather than the one making it inflexible and rigid.

It goes without saying that sexuality is a very delicate issue in most societies, both past and present, and that all religions, ethics, and laws seek to regulate and control it. However, this does not mean that we should not take into consideration the changes that have occurred in the relations between men and women. These changes have reduced the mythic dimension of sexual relations and enabled woman, for the first time in history, to take control of her own body and to choose whether or not to become pregnant. Nor should the execution of a certain penalty, for example the penalty for theft, rely on submission to a divine command beyond time and space. For such penalties are a requirement of society and ethics. They are variable, unstable, and influenced by many different cultural, economic, and political factors.

CHAPTER FIVE

THE SEAL OF PROPHECY

What we can conclude from such examples is that the Mohammedan mission is distinguished by a unique and deeply significant feature. On the one hand, it belongs to what Mohammad Iqbāl calls the "ancient world," not only with regard to its source but also with regard to its inclusion of many aspects of the environment from which it emerged. On the other hand, it belongs to the "modern world," "in so far as the spirit of the revelation is concerned."[89] Moreover, the need for a metaphysical recourse, the existence of many mythic conceptions, the resort to rituals of worship performed in a uniform, stereotypical manner indisputable among the believers,[90] and the corroboration of a number of social values and practices, all reflect a world view that does not differ in essence from the one that prevailed among the Arabs and many other peoples of the world for many centuries. This world view can no longer be imposed on those who have been drastically affected by the new develop-

[89] Mohammad Iqbal, *The Reconstruction of Religious Thought in Islam*, p. 126.

[90] It is worth noting here that what anthropologists call 'rites of passage', such as ᶜAqiqa (the sacrifice on the seventh day after the birth of a child), khafd (circumcision, both male and female) etc. are not mentioned in the Qur'ān, but rather in the collections of ḥadīth. It might be useful to study the history of these practices and inquire whether they reflect something that was prevalent at the time when the Qur'ān was recorded or that already existed at the time of the waḥī.

ments, moral and material, in human civilization. Although history does not stand still, the basic human needs—the need for food, clothes, copulation, and shelter; the need to express feelings, live in a group, and enjoy moral and material security; the need, above all, to bestow on human life and destiny some kind of significance—always remain the same. Nevertheless, there is a great difference between satisfying these needs in a simple, primitive way, and satisfying them in the complicated, sophisticated, and refined ways of the modern world.

The question that urgently arises in this respect, regardless of its exact formulation, is the following: Was it the Mohammedan mission's purpose to set for man limits he cannot transcend? Did it really seek to impose its commands and directives absolutely? Or did it, on the contrary, seek to open wide horizons and to allow man to bear full responsibility for the modes of worship and the organization of all the affairs of life as a free individual, with no supervision save that of his own conscience? Here we must refer to the other side of the mission, which history has effaced and deprived of its creative capacities. It is a side that Muslims have not been used to revealing or exploring with all its obscurities, secrets, and significances, and the very existence of which they do not even realize, not out of slackness or lack of ability, but because their circumstances and the nature of their culture do not allow them to deviate from what they are directed to do.

In this context I find nothing more fitting than Mohammad Iqbal's statement: "In Islam, prophecy reaches its perfection in discovering the need for its own abolition. This involves the keen perception that life cannot forever be kept in leading strings, and that in order to achieve full self-consciousness man must finally be thrown back on his own resources."[91] But is it for Iqbāl or anyone else to determine

[91] Mohammad Iqbāl, *The Reconstruction of Religious Thought in Islam*, p. 126.

this "need for the abolition of prophecy" and to consider its fulfilment as the point where prophecy reaches perfection? Does this not amount to projecting on Islam some notions that are alien to it? The answer to these questions depends on our conception of the idea of "the sealing of prophecy"[92] (khatm al nubuwwa). Does 'Mohammed, the seal of the prophets' mean that he is merely the last of them and that his mission, which came later in time, simply affirms the previous missions and has ascendancy over them?

All we can do here is to analyze the only two logical possibilities whereby this "sealing" can take place:

The first possibility comes to mind most readily, because it is frequently mentioned in Islamic literature and embraced by the majority of Muslims, who imagine it to be the only one. According to this view, prophecy is sealed "from the inside." In other words, he who seals remains within the framework in which he belongs and already exists. In a sense, he is the captive of what he has sealed. There is no way for him to escape or transcend it, just as a man who locks himself in his house remains a prisoner inside. Sealing, in this sense, only indicates a chronological order in which Mohammed comes at the end of the list of prophets and represents the final link in the long chain of prophecy that begins with Adam and ends with Mohammed. If the system that includes the prophet of Islam contained elements in common between him and his predecessors, he was bound to adopt these elements wholly and to be subject to exactly the same conditions as his predecessors. In that sense there was no difference between him and them, or between his

[92] "Mohammed is not the father of any of your men, but he is the Apostle of Allah and the seal of the prophets; and Allah is cognizant of all things" (al-Aḥzāb (The Allies) 33/40). I will not discuss the popular conception of the seal, because the need to translate abstract concepts into concrete things was precisely the reason why the accounts of the Sirat speak of the seal between the prophet's shoulders as one of the signs of prophecy. See Sirat Ibn Isḥāq, p. 69.

mission and theirs. If the prophets before him were sent exclusively to their own peoples, he was sent to the Arabs, and if some of them were kings, like David and Solomon, he too carried the marks of a king, a political ruler, and the founder of a state. If the others were legislators, like Moses, he too produced similar or even better laws, and if they all worked miracles—Moses parting the sea with his rod, Jesus speaking while still in the cradle and bringing back the dead—he too was obliged to work material miracles, such as providing an abundance of food and a profusion of water, healing the sick, having an extraordinary capacity for marriage, etc.[93] In other words, he had to be like them in all their achievements, or indeed surpass them within the same framework and by the same means. The only difference between him and them was that he would not be succeeded by another prophet.[94]

This understanding of the "sealing of prophecy" is not surprising, for people usually compare the new with the familiar and only rarely recognize the originality of the former. To put it differently, they can only think in terms of what already exists and resonates in their minds. However, some things that go beyond the limits of what is thought possible in certain circumstances, and seem impossible to the minds of those who live at a specific time, may nevertheless exist, potentially, so to speak. Their meaning may remain concealed under the thick layers of perception and

[93] The books of Sirat are full of these material miracles that the collective imagination considered indispensable for the completion of prophecy. See Alāqdī ᶜAyyad, *Al Shifa fī al-taᶜrif bi Hoquq al Mustafa* (many editions). Why should this be surprising when similar miracles have been attributed to saints (awliya') and holy men, and called 'karāmāt', even though they differ in no respect whatsoever from those attributed to the prophet?

[94] The Bahā'i embrace this conception, arguing that although prophecy has been sealed, apostles can still appear after Mohammed. That is how they justify their belief in the nineteenth-century founder of their religion. On Baha'ism, see al-Munsif b. ᶜAbed al-Jalil, *Al Firqa al-Hashimiyya fil Islam* (The Hashemite Group in Islam), Tunisia, 1999.

exegesis that have caused them to deviate from their true purposes and objectives. Their latent capacities may be lying in wait for the right circumstances, the suitable environment, the appropriate individuals, so that they may emerge, manifest themselves, and spread in a way that makes one wonder why they remained obscure and unrecognized for so long.

Consider, for example, how Muslims, until very recently, envisioned the holder of political power—whether caliph, king, prince, or emperor—as the kind of man about whom Ibn Khaldūn's aptly said that "there is no power above his." His deeds go unquestioned, and all must obey him, even if he is a tyrant. Then consider how this changed and the public came to realize the necessity of consulting the "citizens," who were formerly thought of as merely the "flock." The utmost attained by Islamic political thought from the Caliphate of Abū Bakr until the last century was what Al Mawardi laid down in the fifth century after the Hegira in his book *al-Aḥkām al-Sultaniyya* about the necessity of the designation of a ruler by council (bay^c^a) only when that position was vacant, and then only with the acquiescence of those who "bind and unbind" (ahl al-ḥall wa al-^c^aqd). Consultation or counsel (*Shūra*) would have been inconceivable under any circumstances other than the vacancy of the office of ruler, even if the person in question was autocratic and dictatorial.[95] Those in our own days who, unlike some leaders of Islamicist organizations, do not reject democracy as being incompatible with Islam with regard to the two verses that mention counsel (*Shūra*)[96]—one in the form of describing a

[95] The behavior of the Ghazz people aroused Ibn Faḍlān's amazement, for "if they agreed on something and resolved to carry it out, the basest and lowest of them can overrule what they had agreed upon." In other words, every individual had the right to object and not only those who have the power to "bind and unbind," as is the case in Islamic countries. *Riḥlat Ibn Faḍlān,* second edition, Damascus, 1977, p. 122.

[96] "And those who respond to their Lord and keep up prayer, and their

practice and the other citing a command by the prophet—as obvious references to consultative rule *(Ḥukm Shūrawī)* and even democracy. They would not have interpreted the Qur'ān in that way, were it not for the modern consciousness, which completely rejects absolute power and wishes to limit and supervise the power of rulers by various institutional means. This example shows that what Muslims overlooked in the past is by no means less legitimate than what they accepted, and can be brought to life without any sense of contrivance or disregard for the inherited viewpoint, once the objective circumstances allowing the emergence of the latent capacities mentioned above are in place.

On this basis, the second possibility of understanding the notion of 'sealing' would be a sealing 'from outside'; that is, the sealing would put an end to man's need to depend on a source of knowledge and a standard of conduct derived from any resources other than his own. This is a declaration of the dawn of a new era for humanity at large; it is the inauguration of a new phase in history, in which man, who has come of age, no longer needs another to guide him or to support him in everything. The prophet's role then would have been to lead man to his new responsibility and to allow him to bear the consequences of his own choices. This would be similar to the case of the man who locks the door of his house—here, the house of prophecy, the house of all prophets—and, sealing it from the outside, is no longer a prisoner, but able to roam the vast land of God. The prophet would have granted man the freedom to live in houses he builds by his own effort, reasoning, and intelligence, by the dictates of his individual and collective interests, and by what enables him to fulfill his humanity and his sublime status in the uni-

---

rule is to take counsel among themselves, and who spend out of what we have given them" (The counsel (ash-Shūra) 42/38); "Pardon them therefore and ask protection for them, and take counsel with them in the affair, so when you have determined, thus place your trust in Allah" (The Family of Imran (Al-i-Imrān) 3/158).

verse. In this case, the prophet would really have been "a herald, a witness, and a harbinger," and a "good example" (ᶜUswa ḥasana) through his deeds and sayings. He would have provided a model of justice, love, mercy, benevolence, and general uprightness in a manner compatible with the circumstances of his own time, rather than strictly and finally underlining what should and should not be done, which would only have reaffirmed the subordination he had come to fight, and merely replaced one form of imitation and mimicry with another.

The message of liberation in Islam is far from the extreme stand taken by later Islamic thought—with the possible exception of the leading mystics—that turns the imitation of the apparent aspects of the prophetic model into the adoption of a fixed legal form and becomes a hollow perpetuation of a rigid structure consisting of imposed will and thought.[97] True freedom can only be arrived at by a thorough understanding of the causes and experiences that determined this model, causing it to adopt one solution and not another. However, since the role of religion involves freeing man from his existential anxiety, assuaging this anxiety by eliminating freedom would only cause man to lead a stagnant life, similar to that of animals inhabiting extremely cold areas, where they cut back all their activities and only exercise their most basic vital functions. In other words, by refraining from action, man would become a passively receptive subject and nothing more. As a result, his best features—his imagination, his creative abilities, his courage to face tyranny, and his freedom of conscience—would be destroyed. To put it differently,

[97] The German theologian Drewermann had in mind the principle of freedom that characterizes Islam and is obscured by the imbrications between religion and politics when he said: "Islamicism is truly a religion of liberty. However, the medieval imbrications of religion and politics in our days often make it appear as a principle contrary to liberty," E. Drewermann, *Fonctionnaires de Dieu*, Paris, 1993, p. 732.

all that represents the strength of a free personality and that raises man above the other creatures would be lost.

It is true that man in his search for truth is like a blind person who can only perceive the characteristics of things that fall within the scope of his other senses, and it is also true that religion–Islam par excellence–is the language through which man, as much as he possibly can, conceives the purpose of being. Nevertheless, nothing can substitute for personal experience of the values that deserve every risk on man's part in the attempt to realize them in cooperation his fellow humans. Nothing can replace that experience, be it the forms of an inherited religion, the precepts of a certain institution, or the mindless imitation of a model in purely worldly matters, such as clothing, even if the model were the prophet himself, let alone Imams and holy men, whether dead or alive.

Through that experience, Mohammed, the son of Abdullah, would have sealed prophecy, putting an end to repetition and regurgitation, and opening up the possibility of a future built by man and his fellow-men under the aegis of personal freedom, individual responsibility, and creative cooperation. Through that experience, he would have established the pillars of a truly universal ethic, and his role would not have been restricted to presenting ready-made prescriptions for Muslims to apply passively and mechanically.

I am almost beginning to hear voices condemning this conception of 'sealing': Have Muslims all over the world and through the ages concurred in error and aberration? What would remain of Islam if Muslims were to cease what they have been practicing up to now? But, wait! Let us put aside the moral and material interests that may motivate these critics in their desire to keep things as they are, despite the crisis of credibility afflicting traditional religiousness in modern societies, and let us also put aside the heavy burden of the past and the powerful impact of inheritance. Who, then, has the right to speak in the name of the true Islam? Since when have the products of scholars been an expression of what lies in the hearts of Muslims in general? Do they share God's knowledge of "what is in the breasts"? How do they know that Muslims in the future will not adopt a deeper and better understanding than the one that has existed for less than fourteen centuries, a relatively short period of time in comparison with the long life of humanity?

And again, weren't human beings called upon to travel the earth and behold God's creation? Once they took this call seriously, they realized that God spoke to them through the 'symphony of creation', in which they participate as the only creatures capable of enriching it with the spontaneous ideas of their imagination and the organized ideas of their minds. Nothing can replace humans in that role, because they alone are able to add a melody to the voices of the world, if they listen carefully to what abides in the depths of their souls and to the loud or silent chant of existence. Likewise, nothing can stop the search of humans for the best and the most beneficial means of organizing their lives and achieving happiness. Thus, the Muslim has every reason to take pride in the fact that the Mohammedan mission, as a matter of principle, urges him to seek that happiness, by responding to new developments and not just following the example of his fathers, by venturing into the rich field of experience and not just resorting to a ready-made list of slogans to be repeated like the braying of a donkey under its load, and by bringing the young up on independence of thought, rather than training them like animals to turn to heaps of memorized phrases.

It has become the habit of Catholic theologians, particularly since the Second Vatican Council, to justify the Church's re-examination of its past conduct and its sometimes abominable mistakes as a sign of growth and deepening understanding, rather than as a repudiation of the past, which would destroy any belief in the infallibility of the Church.[98] Islam, fortunately, recognizes no clergy and there-

[98] One example is the case of Galileo and the Catholic Church's ac-

fore is not disconcerted, either in principle or in practice, when its adherents sin, whether the number of sinners is small or large. Nor is there anything to prevent us admitting that the exegesis adopted by one or more generations was suitable for certain cultural and historical circumstances, but must be disregarded and avoided in others. This applies to both Sunni and Shi'ite thought. For they both treat the Muslim as if he were a minor in need of a second round of supervision—the round of the guardianship (wilāya)—and of the continuation of the waḥi through Imams and Awliyā' (holy men), whose features change but whose prophetic task remains the same. This approach in fact only corresponds to the superficial meaning of 'sealing prophecy': it strictly adheres to the letter of the text and demands submission to the legal precepts (aḥkām) inferred from it by men of the second century after the Hegira, thus considering the Muslim incapable of inferring them himself.[99] Both cases are clear deviations from the divine purpose of 'sealing prophecy'. They both keep man in a state of dependency on leaders, under whatever names and titles, and they both arise from the fear of allowing man to take up the responsibility assigned to him by the Mohammedan mission, and the fear of absolute equality between humans with respect to their rights and duties.

For all these reasons I do not hesitate to assert that the Mohammedan mission inevitably took the demands of its time into consideration, but was ahead of, and beyond, the intellectual and social propensities of its contemporaries in

---

knowledgement of the principle of the freedom of belief, which it had fiercely attacked earlier. It also seems that the Church is slowly beginning to express, somewhat discreetly, its regret over its silent and passive attitude to the Nazi persecution of the Jews. Of course, we are still waiting to hear about the Church's views on its past support of slavery and imperialism, whether in Latin America or in Africa.

[99] On scholars and "holy men" in the Sunni system, see ᶜAbdelmajid Sharfi, "*al Mu'asasa ad-Dīnīyya fil Islam*" (The Religious Institutions in Islam), in *Labanat*, pp. 69-84.

terms of its principal and final purpose. While it was pregnant with possibilities, they only grasped what was closest to the general intellectual standards of the time. The contemporaries of the mission should not be blamed for the outcome of their exegesis. Rather, the blame falls on those who stop at that juncture and who ignore modern man's need for spiritual nurture transcending a mere mechanical submission and absolute obedience to commands and prohibitions. The blame falls on those who disregard the development of 'public space',[100] from a time when everybody had an equal or almost equal chance of reaching the few uniform sources of knowledge, and when debates and disputes focused on the same fairly simple subjects, to a time characterized by the infinite diversity of such sources, ever since the unprecedented spread of education in large sectors of society, the ubiquitous availability of books, magazines, and newspapers, and the rapid, or indeed momentary, transmission of visual and acoustic information, regardless of its nature and source, to any place on the face of the earth, particularly after the internet's invasion of public and private life.

The discrepancy between the mission on the one hand and its applications on the other will only be revealed if we analyze samples of its manifestations after the prophet's death, and their consequences in history, which is the focus of Part Two of this study.

[100] See J. Habermas, *L'espace public* (The Public Space), Paris, 1978 (translation of the German original *Strukturwandel der Öffentlichkeit*). The 'public space', in Habermas's view, is a symbolic space in which the public mind advances, regardless of sectarian or individual interests.

PART TWO

INTRODUCTION TO PART TWO

THE MISSION IN HISTORY

In this part I am not concerned with the historical events in themselves, even though what befell the Muslims after the Prophet's death and throughout the Rashidun and Ummayid reigns is definitely still in need of critical study.[101] The information available on the first century after the Prophet was not recorded until about the middle of the second. It lacks comprehensiveness and is influenced by the disputes in which all the parties were involved, either actively through support or opposition or passively through acquiescence and silence. However, my aim in the study of these events is to arrive at an answer to the following question: if what I have said about the nature of the Mohammedan mission is true, why was it not applied by the first Muslims? Why did the prophet's companions, successors, and all the later generations that followed in their footsteps only adopt solutions that today seem reductive, unsatisfactory, not to say false?

The discrepancy between the supposed aims of the mis-

[101] There is a great difference between the kind of criticism that aims at a better understanding and the one that is based on tribal views and denies Islam any distinctiveness or tries to force it into patterns derived from the history of Christianity and Judaism, for example, by claiming that the Qur'ān was not completed until the third century after the hegira. See P. Crone & M. Cook, *Hagarism. The Making of the Islamic World*, London, 1977; and J. Wansbrough, *Quranic Studies; Sources and Methods of Scriptural Interpretation*, Oxford, 1977.

sion and their outcome in history is not exceptional, but seems to be the rule for all religious and philosophical movements. This is what happened to the Protestant movement and its "companion," Modernity, in which some of the effects of the Reformation proved to be very far removed from, and at times the very opposite of, what the pioneers of the movement had intended.[102] This is also what resulted from the application of Marxism in the Soviet Union. It is quite evident that we cannot approach this issue at the level of intentions, for the Muslims did what they did with a clear conscience, believing that they were being faithful to the demands of the new religion. Their behavior was characterized by absolute spontaneity and did not come under the rule of theories and authorities until long after the death of the first generation.

Although it may never be possible to discover exactly what preoccupied all or some Muslims at the time of the mission, it is certain that the perfection and infallibility that have been attributed to them bear no relation to the historical reality. These characteristics were asserted by the political and religious leaders who were in need of the power and influence provided by such concepts. The history books swarm with accounts of the early Muslims' indulgence in bloody disputes and the scramble for treasures and worldly pleasures (women, slaves, palaces).[103] However, this was only natural and to be expected, because new values—which always need time to take root and to overcome and replace the inherited values—are only manifested gradually and in a manner compatible with the prevailing social conditions.

[102] See M. Weber, *L'Ethique protestante et l'esprit du capitalisme*, Paris, 1985, p. 102; and Ernst Troeltsch, *Protestantisme et Modernité*, Paris, 1991.

[103] Khalil Abd el-Karim, in his work ***Shadū al-Rabāba bi Aḥwāl Mujtama*^c^ *al-Ṣaḥābah***, 3 vols., Cairo, 1997, has collected many accounts from the Sira and Tabakat, in an attempt to reveal the discrepancies between the real image of the first generation and the idealistic image usually presented by the Muslim imagination.

Chapter Six

THE PROPHET'S CALIPHATE

Let us consider the theoretical possibilities for the materialization of the mission in the real social and political circumstances after the prophet's death:

1. First, we note that at that moment in history (after Mohammed's death), it was no longer possible to go back to what things were like in Ḥijāz before the mission. The Islamic call had created a new situation in both Ḥijāz and the Arab Peninsula, which made the tribal system incapable of responding to the bonds forged by Islam between individuals and groups, particularly since that system had begun to show symptoms of disintegration, even before Mohammed arrived with his mission, and a strong desire for a different system, even though the precise nature of that desire was not yet obvious. That is why the establishment of some kind of central rule became inevitable and the chances of the Quraysh playing a central role in political life after the prophet were very good, owing to their status among the Arabs, their past, and their economic weight. Thus, we can explain the apostasy movements that spread among the non-Ḥijāzi tribes during the reign of Abū Bakr as a mere clinging to a disintegrating tribal system overcome by events. In other words, these movements were condemned to failure right from the outset, regardless of the manner in which they were dealt with or of the role played by some individuals in hastening their end.

2. The adoption of the mission by the rich Quraysh, who had at first resisted it, also seemed unlikely, particularly because of that initial resistance. Nevertheless, the course of events shows that the Umayyads in fact adopted the mission, once time had thrown a veil over their past, and the need for their administrative experience, economic strength, and maneuvering ability in a vast Empire of diverse races and conflicting interests had emerged.

3. The same analysis applies to the third possibility, which is the return to what may be called the 'Ṣaḥīfa system' or the non- religious covenant between the immigrant Meccans and the inhabitants of Yathrib/Al Madina, the al 'Aws, the al Khazraj, and the Jews.[104] This system was necessary when the first Muslim group was still weak and the issues had not yet been settled by the expulsion of the Jews, the opening of Mecca, and the Arab tribes' adoption of Islam. When the weakness of the Muslims turned into strength, with the Islamic principles being applied in a large number of domains and religious affiliation becoming the basis for social harmony, this 'Ṣaḥīfa system' was no longer justified.

4. The events of the *Saqīfa* (the meeting held at the hall (*saqīfa*) of bani Sāᶜida after the prophet's death) indicate that there was a possibility of a dangerous division among the Muslims. The immigrants (*Muhājirūn*), who believed that the Quraysh were most worthy of rule after the prophet's death, saw the meeting of the Ansar (the 'helpers' in the Madina) as an attempt to exclude them; as ᶜUmar said: "they come with the intention of preventing us from practising this matter (the caliphate) and depriving us of it." The Ansar, for their part, took the view expressed in the words of their khatīb (orator): "We are Allah's Ansār and the majority of the Mus-

[104] See the text of this covenant, which some call "the Constitution of the Madina" in Ibn Hisham, *The Life of Muhammad: A Translation of Ibn Iṣḥāq's Sirat Rasul Allah*, London and New York: Oxford University Press, 1955, 231-233. There have been many studies on this covenant, some asserting its authenticity and others denying it.

lim army, while you emigrants are a small group." The only compromise the Ansar were willing to make was sharing power: "One ruler from us and one ruler from you." But ᶜUmar created a surprise by his 'prompt and sudden action' when he hastened to pledge his allegiance (*bayᶜa*) to Abū Bakr, thus creating an accomplished fact after taking advantage of the struggle between the tribes of Aws and Khazraj. Haunted by the specter of dispute over who should rule, he said: "We are afraid that if we left the people, they might pledge their allegiance after us to one of their men, in which case we would have given them our consent for something against our real wish or we would have opposed them and caused great trouble."[105]

5. The fifth possibility was that of the rule falling to *Ahl al Bayt* (the prophet's family) represented by ᶜAli and al-ᶜAbbas. In that case, the ruler would have combined the symbolic authority of being a blood relation of the prophet and the temporal authority that was the subject of the dispute. ᶜAli's character in particular might have made him a suitable candidate, but it seems that there was an aversion to the principle of combining authorities, as this would have created an unchallengeable power, which would have been very hard to oppose in any matter, however weighty or trivial. The Arabs were neither used to this kind of power, nor willing to put up with it, however representative of the most transcendent levels of legitimacy it may have seemed to be to the Shi'ites.

6. Thus, the possibility that became the reality benefited from the weakness of the other alternatives, but it was the elements of age, experience, and personal enlightenment that played the decisive role in the assignment of the Caliphate of the prophet to Abū Bakr according to the tribal traditions. His standing among Muslims made it very hard for any of his competitors to disparage him, and his participation in

[105] Saḥīḥ al-Bukhārī, the Book of Hudūd (penalties).

the Quraysh council (Nadwa), the institution from which the Arab state was later to develop, secured him the support of the rich Quraysh. As a result of his exploits in the apostasy (*ar-ridda*) wars, the pre-eminence enjoyed by the Quraysh on the Peninsula before Islam was accepted, and all the tribes that recognized their leadership rallied round them.

In this context, it is important to make two essential observations. The first is that in choosing Abū Bakr religious considerations were either completely absent or very secondary. His seniority in Islam and his leading of prayers (Imamate) during the prophet's illness were only mentioned later for purposes of justification. Moreover, the statement of his caliphate in the text (*tanṣīṣ*) was brought up in some Sunni circles later and only in response to the Shi'ite claim of the caliphate for Ali. Choosing the person who was to lead the group was a purely worldly matter, and a vital necessity called for by the vacancy of the ruling position, which Mohammed had occupied unrivalled. It was merely an application of the universal social law whereby every society, whether small or large, needs a ruler and representative, to prevent chaos and the disruption of the orderly life of the society.[106] Accordingly, since the time of Abū Bakr, Islam—having emerged in an environment without states—has fused with the state to such an extent that its continuing existence could no longer be envisioned without the continuing existence of the state. This development, of course, has carried with it a fossilizing of both the history and the vitality of the Islamic mission.

The second observation is that the appointment of Abū Bakr to that position—like that of the caliphs, kings, princes, and sultans who came after him—was not a matter for all Muslims, men and women, rich and poor, masters, slaves,

[106] This is the essence of what theorists of the Caliphate as an Islamic ruling system had in mind when they cited the pre-Islamic line of verse: "those who lack a wise leader cannot reform disorder."

patrons, and clients,[107] but only for the leaders and possessors of power, later described in the literature of *Aḥkām Sultāniyya* (constitutional and administrative law) as those who have the power to "bind and unbind" (*Ahl al Ḥall wal ᶜAqd*). The ruler was unable to rule, if they did not support him and accept his authority, or at least refrain from dissenting. As a result, from the moment of the prophet's death, the sense of equality among all Muslims began to fade. The values that had prevailed before it resurfaced, obscuring the revolutionary spirit of the new religion. In other words, a democratic electoral system, as we understand it today, was inconceivable because it was beyond the Muslims' mental horizons at the time. This system is a product of the progress undergone by humanity only in the last two or three centuries. It is related to religion only to the extent that religion can either be used for mystification or carry the potential of demystification. The latent principles of religion remain hidden waiting for the right circumstances, so that they may come to the fore and materialize in historical living reality. If *shūra* was limited to a small number of people and later restricted even further, being almost effaced by hereditary succession and the ascendancy of the powerful, this did not happen through

[107] Al-Jaḥiz says: "We presume that the general public does not know the meaning of the Imamate or the Caliphate and does not differentiate between its existence or the lack of it, but rather follows the prevailing fashions and is swept along by the currents. It may feel more comfortable with the unjust than the just. The general public is a tool used by the elite to accomplish tasks, pursue interests, and fill in gaps" ("Uthmāniyya," in *Rasa'il Al-Jaḥīz*, Cairo, 1979, 4/36). We find echoes of this in Mohammad Abdu's comment: "What the progress and enlightenment of a nation depends on is the majority of its middle classes and leaders, not the general public or laity. For if the minds and perceptions of the men of the middle classes and those above them are sound, the nation will progress. Once the upper classes are in their proper place, the ignorance or superstition of the public cannot obstruct the nation's advancement and civilization." Mohammad Abduh, *Al-Aᶜmāl al Kāmilah* (The Complete Works), second edition, vol. 2, p. 160.

Islam. Rather, religion was used to legitimize and justify the ruling system, and the standard of religious consciousness, as in all ruling systems, was determined by the extent to which the system responded to the principles of the prophetic mission, on which the religion was based. It is obvious that this standard has changed and developed, and that in the twenty-first century its relation to the political system differs drastically from what it was in the seventh century.

Moreover, the theoretical possibilities of filling the gap caused by the prophet's death were many and their chances of being realized uneven. The actual outcome was not necessarily the most compatible with the logic of the mission, and was, in the final analysis, determined by the historical circumstances. Two other large spheres of social life have been subject to similar factors, which caused them to drift away from the spirit of the mission. I shall discuss these two spheres together, because they are both related to the sublime human and Qur'ānic value of human dignity.

The first sphere is that of the slaves. Although the phenomenon of slavery has now become a thing of the past, this does not prevent us from questioning the reasons that led Muslims, for centuries, to enslave their brothers and sisters, ignoring the call of the revelation. The Qur'ān, which states that God honors all humans without distinction, lists the occasions on which slaves should be liberated, and which should in practice have led to the abolition of slavery as a whole. It is also noteworthy that the Qur'ān mentions no situation that may lead to the enslavement of one human being by another, whether in war or in peace. Yet, the "Conquests" created a source for new slaves, with the Arab masters using the males for all kinds of strenuous tasks and exploiting the females without mercy. The logic of the mission, which aimed at a gradual and realistic approach to the existing situation, was forgotten, and Muslims handled slavery in the manner of non-Muslims or of the pre-Islamic era (*Jahilīyya*), or even worse. At this level, the dictates of avaricious worldly interests prevented a consistent interpretation of the mission, and Muslims missed the opportunity of being the first to call for Human Rights in a general sense and to apply them in front of all the peoples of the world, who at that time saw no harm in some people lacking freedom. At best, jurists urged Muslims to treat their slaves well in much the same way as they called for animal rights.

The second sphere is that of women. Here too, Muslims were no innovators among the nations, in which the notion of the inferiority of women had been ingrained since ancient times. The "other sex" had always been a synonym for weakness, evil, and comradeship with the devil. Moreover, even the purely physiological phenomenon of menstruation was thought of by most peoples as a sign of woman's contamination throughout her period. As a result, she was not allowed near the food of others and could even be isolated.[108] Wasn't she created out of Adam's bent rib? Wasn't she the one who seduced him to eat from the tree, which was the first "sin" and the reason for the fall from heaven? The Qur'ān excludes these two "myths" mentioned in the Book of Genesis. It insists that all human beings were created out of the same spirit and that God created woman so that man might find peace of mind with her. It further states clearly that the seduction was by Satan and not Eve, and that God forgave Adam, thereby absolving him from the sin. However, instead of reflecting on the Qur'ān's exclusion, Muslims vied with each other in referring to the *Israeliyyāt* in an attempt to muster support for their tribal view of woman, and to interpret the Qur'ān "with an authority not sent down by Allah" in a manner that erased all the essential differences between Mohammed's mission and *Ahl al Kitāb*'s pronouncements on

[108] See The Old Testament, The Book of Leviticus, XV/19-33. G. Durand points out that the Sabbath was originally celebrated once a month at what was thought to be the period of the moon goddess Ishtar (the name cAisha is derived from Ishtar), rather than once a week. The word Sabbath is derived from a root meaning "Ishtar's bad day." G. *Durand, Les structures anthropologiques de l'imaginaire*, p. 119.

this issue. They failed to rise to the level of the mission's noble aims and to realize that Islam's characteristic feature was its establishment of values that broke the bonds with the prevailing heritage. Even worse, they envisioned Islam according to their desires, needs, and interests, until it became synonymous with women's oppression, degradation, and confinement in the home behind thick walls. As a result, Islam became responsible for depriving women of the most basic rights, such as the right to work and learn, and was used to create an unstable identity that sought to express itself by forcing deluded young girls to wear the veil.[109] Here too, Muslims missed the chance of being pioneers in acknowledging the absolute equality of men and women. Women's seizure of some of their rights—which they have been able to do only in a few Muslim countries—was achieved against the Muslims' will, rather than with their help, as should have been the case, had they truly understood the deeper logic of the mission. This compels me to investigate the historical factors that caused this deviation.

These factors are numerous and hard to separate or distinguish with regard to their importance. Some of them—such as the pre-Islamic mental habits which persisted either in the Arabs themselves or in Muslims of other races adher-

[109] The two verses arbitrarily used for the purpose are: "Oh, Prophet! Say to your wives and your daughters and the women of the believers that they let down upon them their over-garments; this will be more proper, that they may be known, and thus they will not be given trouble, and Allah is forgiving and merciful" (Al-Aḥzāb (The Allies) 33/59); "and let them wear their head coverings over their bosoms" (An-Nūr (the light) 24/31). The first verse only enjoins women to let down their over-garments so that they may be recognized and not hurt when they go out at night to answer a call of nature in the cities where houses have no toilets. The second verse only tries to prevent women revealing their charms, by asking them to cover their chests, so that their breasts may not be revealed through the opening of their shirts. How far both verses are from the judgments of the jurists who think that the whole female body is a pudendum!

ing to the cultures and religions that prevailed in the regions conquered by Islam—are cultural. Those who embraced the new religion did not start with a clean slate, but brought with them their own opinions, sentiments, and values. As is to be expected, they understood the Mohammedan mission and interpreted what was new and original in the new text with reference to their customary way of thinking. Thus, in many issues, they projected on Islam concerns that were alien or indeed opposed to its spirit and its purpose. Moreover, the first Muslim generation's knowledge of nature and its laws, of man and his psychology, and of society and its rules played a crucial role in their understanding of the teaching of their religion, which in time took on a certain sanctity that is very hard to eliminate or overcome as knowledge progresses, develops and cancels its earlier stages.

Other factors are political and related to the dictates of governing the affairs of a group of people in a certain environment. Since the tribal system prevailed in the Arab Peninsula, the individuals charged with responsibility for the affairs of the Islamic community and the appointed rulers could hardly be expected to create a new approach that was not already known to the Arabs. That is why the four Rashidun caliphs and the early Umayyad kings behaved as tribal leaders would have done, despite the fact that their power extended to matters that differed in type from what would have fallen under a tribal Sheikh's rule, and to territories that were by far larger than those in which a tribe would typically reside. It is well-known that blood bonds are of great importance in tribal ethics, and their importance remained undiminished under Islamic rule, with non-Arabs being denied the rights and privileges enjoyed by Arabs. Thus, Muslims of Arab origin seized the highest political and military positions in the nascent Empire and the 'mawālī' (subjects converted to Islam) and all Muslims of non-Arab origin in general were excluded. Their resulting resentment made them an easy prey for any rebellious movements that aspired to take power. It was also the reason why they—the

Persians in particular—nurtured the *shu^c^ubiyyah*[110] tendency as a reaction to this exclusion. Similarly, many of the excluded non-Arabs (again Persians in particular) would later strive to excel over Arabs in fields such as the sciences—of religion, language, etc.—that the Arabs looked down on.

The political factors are connected with the demands of building a state. A state can only be founded on a set of institutions, however primitive and simple these may be, and it cannot last unless it is directed and guided on the basis of rules and standards agreed upon—be it only implicitly—by the rulers and the ruled. Thus, it was natural that the institutions and standards in question were borrowed in the first place from the Meccan experience that preceded Islam. However, due to the limited nature of this experience and its inapplicability within a framework that included races with different cultures and went beyond the tribal system with its simple components, it was necessary to inoculate them with the neighboring nations' experience of dealing with aides and agents, money and taxes, and landed or other property. Thus, the running of the nascent Empire[111] required the in-

[110] al-Shu^c^ubiyyah is a movement in early Muslim society that denied a privileged position to Arabs. (Translator's note)

[111] Empire is an ancient form of state in most cultures, and is characterized above all by its indefinite borders, which expand at times of strength and contract at times of weakness. In an empire, diverse languages, cultures, and religions exist side by side. Thus, its citizens are not all subject to one and the same law, as has been the case since the rise of the modern nation state with its firmly established borders. In all probability, the main reason for the crisis in contemporary Islamic thought is its failure to comprehend or internalize the crucial changes to the form of states, kingdoms, and princedoms. Despite the disappearance of the Empire's basic components it continues to adhere to some of the past features, such as a jurisprudence designed for the followers of one religion who do not necessarily live under the rule of one state and its positive laws, which pay no regard to their religion even if they are influenced by a specific religious heritage. There is no doubt that the institutional structure of the modern state and its ability to coerce and to intervene in all domains by far surpasses the structures of the states of old.

troduction of the "diwan al cAtaa'" (record or register of charity) to keep account of the names of debtors and their debts, which memory alone could not retain. Later on, similar registers were sent to the army, the postal and construction services, and all other services and utilities necessary for any centralized rule. In none of these organizations did the Muslims feel the need for any religious considerations; rather, they resorted to experiments that led to the adaptation of the already existing systems and to innovations that preserved the different social balances. This is evident in the different ruling systems of the conquered regions and is also reflected in the fact that cUmar refrained from distributing the Sawād region[112] in Iraq among the participants of the raid on it.

However, the institutions founded by man always need to be justified to those who benefit from as well as those who submit to them. Once they are in existence a supporting authority is sought, and the natural source of such support at that time was religion. We can safely assume that the motivation of the Muslims' political decisions was practical rather than Islamic, even if at times it appeared to approach the principles of the Mohammedan mission.

Economic factors also played a highly significant role in the first Muslim generation's deviation from the mission at the level of interpretation as well as of practical implementation. For, with the exception of the great merchants of Mecca, almost all the inhabitants of the peninsula, Bedouins and urbanites alike, suffered from poverty due to the climate of their environment and the lack of natural resources. Such was their condition before Islam, and it remained so during the days of the prophet and Abū Bakr. However, once cUmar b. Khattāb, a man of profound insight, had come to power, he realized that the best way to overcome the antagonisms

[112] Al-Sawād is a name used in early Islamic times for Iraq. 'Sawād' means black in Arabic and was applied to southern Iraq due to its viridity, which contrasted with the light colors of the desert to which the Arabs were accustomed. (Translator's note)

among the followers of the new religion and the enmities resulting from the "civil war," which had occupied Abū Bakr, was to divert the conflicting energies towards an external enemy. Although this was a classical solution in such cases, his swift action, relying on the element of surprise, succeeded beyond all expectation, which was all the more surprising since the balance of forces favored the two great powers of the time, Persia and Byzantium. These two enemy powers did not anticipate being threatened by the Arabs, who were known for their fragmented social structure. They did not recognise the radical change caused by Islam, whether at the psychological level or at the level of religious bonds, which transcend all tribal ties.

The astounding promptness and relative ease with which the conquests during the reign of ᶜUmar took place, were unprecedented in history. Syria and Egypt were seized from Byzantine rule, and the Persian Empire in Iraq and Persia was completely eradicated. What distinguishes these conquests from those of Alexander the Great, who invaded vast areas, is that their influence persisted after ᶜUmar's death. It did not even fade away when the rule passed to his successors, and the victories continued in Africa, in particular Morocco, the Iberian Peninsula, and southern Europe, for almost a whole century. As far as the present study is concerned, two main issues arise in connection with these conquests.

The first issue is that of the booty the Muslim Arabs gained as a result of their invasion of countries rich in natural resources, crafts, industries, and ancient civilizations, which went beyond anything they expected or could have dreamt of in their destitute peninsula.[113] The direct conse-

[113] Cf. the following account: "Abu Hurayra reported on his visits from Bahrain to ᶜUmar: I found him at prayer and I saluted him, whereupon he asked me about the people and said: 'What have you brought?' I said: 'Five hundred thousand.' He said: 'Do you realize what you are saying?' I said: 'A hundred and a hundred' until I reached five. He said: 'You are sleepy, go back to your people and sleep. Come back to me in the morn-

quence of this was the rise of a *nouveau riche* class, consisting of the heads of the Quraysh houses who organised and led the conquests, and a number of individuals who stood out among the Ansārs (helpers). As could be expected, the "treasure of gold and silver" that the mission had rejected grew drastically, and provoked the resistance of Abi Dhar al Ghafārī and other men like him, whose Islamic feelings were offended by the inequalities between Muslims. For, a minority of them possessed the vast fertile lands that yielded great wealth, which was evident in their large houses, their expensive clothes, their many male and female slaves, their extensive stocks of cattle, and other aspects of their lifestyle. These were the likes of Abdel Raḥmān b. ᶜAouf, al-Zubair b. ᶜAuwām, and Talḥa b. ᶜUbaid Allah.[114] At the same time, the majority of the Arabs and non-Arabs who had embraced Islam lived in hard economic circumstances and did not enjoy the booties of the conquests or any other benefits, such as donations, land, a share in the development of the means of trade, or income derived from holding governmental positions in the different regions of the caliphate.

However, the effect of the conquest went beyond financial matters, creating, as it did, a utilitarian mindset or, rather, perpetuating the pre-Islam mentality of the rich Quraysh, in

---

ing.' I returned next morning and he said: 'What have you brought?' I said: 'Five hundred.' He said: 'Is that true?' I said: 'Yes, I am sure.' So he said to the people: 'He has brought to us a lot of money. If you wish we can count it or if you wish we can weigh it'." Aḥmad b. Yeḥya Al-Balathuri, *Futuḥ Al-Buldān*, pp. 439–440.

[114] These facts are well-known and need not be repeated in detail. Accounts are found in the compilation of the biographies of the Prophet's companions such as al-*Istīᶜāb* by Ibn Abdel Bar, *'Usd al-Ghābah* by Ibn al-'Athīr, al-*'Isābah* by Ibn Hajar, in the books of history, and other sources. The men concerned not only amassed treasure, but also deviated morally from Islamic values, as in the case of Khālid b. al-Walīd, who killed Mālik b. Nuwaira al-Tamīmī and falsely accused him of apostasy, so that he could then marry his victim's beautiful wife without even waiting to make sure that she was not pregnant by her deceased husband.

which the ends justified the means. Moreover, the conquests established social relationships founded on patronage, obedience, and submission of the weak to the strong, thus denying the relationships based on equality and justice that Islam tried to introduce. And since the reverse side of obedience is rejection and rebellion, it would not be surprising if the seeds of the rebellious and secessionist movements that have marked Islamic history since the reign of ᶜUthmān were first sown in that period. All this was to have so great an influence on the later juristic, scholastic and moral theories that scholars were prepared to adopt Persian values and invoke the lives of the Chosroes (kings of Persia), as if there were no difference between them, on the one hand, and the mission with its religious demands, on the other.[115] Furthermore, the ordinance of obedience (*Nizām at-tāᶜa*) was to have its influence on social education, since successive Muslim generations would be raised to submit to the will of others instead of developing the values of mutual respect and the ethics of freedom and responsibility, which would lead them to obey willingly the social rules, as long as these rules could be changed by democratic means.[116]

The second issue that concerns me regarding the conquests is their legitimacy according to the logic of the Mission. It may seem strange even to mention this issue, since Muslims in the invaded countries have come to consider what happened to their ancestors as an act of grace that enlightened them and guided them from their blinding error to the right path. I do not, of course, raise this issue from that perspective, but simply wonder whether the Arab invasion of

[115] Al-Mawerdi's book *Adab al-Dunia wal Dīn* (Cairo, many editions) gives a good account of this phenomenon.

[116] The latter kind of education is advocated by the Swiss psychiatrist Jean Piaget, and discussed by Hisham Sharabi in his recent work, *al-Nizām al Abawi wa Ishkaliyat Takhaluf al-Mujtamaᶜ al-ᶜArabi* (Patriarchy and the Problem of the Backwardness of Arab Society), second edition, Beirut, pp. 62-63.

the countries concerned—with the invaders imprisoning the men, taking the women as concubines, and exploiting the natural resources—was 'Jihād' in the Qu'rānic sense, or simply a military requirement for building their Empire under the pretext of spreading Islam. In other words, does the religious mission need violence in order to guide people? A brief glance at the map of the Islamic world shows that about three-fifths of all Muslims live in countries—including Indonesia, China, and large parts of India and black Africa—that embraced Islam without violence, through trade, scholarship, and the adoption of the Sufi ways. This clearly indicates that Islam needs no violence in order to spread, and that the war waged by the first Muslims against their neighbors was in reality motivated by purely worldly interests. Rather than referring to this war in objective terms such as occupation, invasion, or imperialism—as it might be understood in modern times—they considered it a 'Jihad' (Holy War) for God's cause, in which they executed His will and followed the teaching of His prophet. In other words, Mohammed's conquests were understood to be offensive invasions of the same kind as those carried out by Muslims after his death. This analogy bestowed on their actions a legitimacy they would never have acquired otherwise. That is why a stance like that of Sufiyan ath-Thawri, who thought that "fighting the heathens was not obligatory unless they started first, but then it would become mandatory,"[117] was

[117] Mohammad b. Abi Sahl Al-Sarakhsi, *Sharḥ as-Siyar al-Kabīr*, Hydarabād, 1355 of the hijra, vol. 1, pp. 125–126. Sufyan ath-Thawri's stance is based on the following two verses: "But if they do fight you, then slay them" (the Cow 2/191); "Fight the polytheists all together as they fight you all together" (Chapter of Immunity 9/36). However, al-Sarakhsi comments that the call to jihad was revealed to Mohammed gradually. First the prophet was commanded to convey the mission and avoid the heathens. Then he was prompted to "dispute with them in the best manner." Subsequently Muslims were allowed to fight, but only if the heathens attacked them. Eventually they were commanded to fight, except during the sacred months, and finally they were commanded to fight

considered odd and accepted neither by jurists nor by politicians.

By stating this historical fact I do not deny that those who carried out the conquests believed that they were doing the right thing and that they were merely fulfilling what the prophet himself had set out to do. Nor do I deny that many of those "conquerors" sacrificed their lives and their possessions for God's cause, aspiring only to a reward in the Hereafter. Nevertheless, this must not obscure the other side and the real, hidden motives behind the conquests, which clearly deviated from the purposes of the mission by granting 'jihad' in its offensive and violent form, together with all the corruption it brings,[118] superiority over freedom of belief and persuasion by means of "what is best." Had the spread of Islam not been accompanied by violence and exploitation, it might have taken on a different, more positive tinge and made a greater and deeper impact, with less reliance on states, governments, institutions of *ḥisba* (state intervention), and intellectual or even physical terrorism! In saying this, I do not wish to beat a futile retreat into history or to sit in judgment over our ancestors, but rather to de-sanctify human history and recognize both the virtues and faults, without exaggeration, mystification and obfuscation.

---

without any qualification. al-Sarakhsi's account represents the prevalent exegesis, which justifies aggression.

[118] Al-Sarakhsi mentions al-Uzaʿi's view that "it is not permissible for the Muslims to wreck and pillage in the 'war territories' or the conquered regions because that would be corruption and God does not like corruption," and he comments: "if it were proven that encouraging construction is a laudable thing and encouraging destruction is an abhorrent thing then we would say: if killing souls has been permitted, and it is the gravest of things, then everything lesser than that, such as destroying buildings and cutting down trees, is most probably also allowed," *Sharḥ as-Siyar al-Kabīr*, vol. 1, p. 35.

CHAPTER SEVEN

INSTITUTIONALIZING RELIGION

Like other religions and doctrines, Islam was subjected to the requirements of organization and institutionalization. The principles carried by the mission could not have materialized in history, and particularly in the seventh century, had they not answered such requirements. Institutionalization is in fact the transition from theory to practice, from what exists potentially to what exists actually. In this transition the principles inevitably lose part of their power and acquire certain particularities dictated by the characteristics, divergences, and contradictions of reality. Thus, it is quite understandable that a certain exegesis, from among the many that are theoretically possible or that actually exist and have been adopted by individuals or groups, will gain ascendancy over others. Such an exegesis will gradually acquire the character of truthfulness, correctness, and intuitiveness because it most befits people's mentality and the balance of social, political, and economic powers at a specific time. The institutionalization of Islam is manifested in three ways:

First, it is manifested in the differences between Islam and other religions, and between Muslims and other human groups, such as polytheists, Ahl al Kitāb (those who possess a Holy Scripture) and others. This is not surprising because Muslims were a minority among the peoples of the invaded region and they were afraid of merging with the neighboring religious and racial elements. Thus, it was necessary for them to create ways in which they could easily recognize each other, for instance by their clothing, food, and their conduct in general. The Muslims' desire to remain distinct expresses itself in the many rules known as the ᶜUmarian stipulations[119]—including the obligation imposed on Ahl al Dhimmah (the people of the covenant) to wear a special kind of overcoat (*al ghīyār*) or precluding them from horseriding, building churches or purchasing property—regardless of how accurate this reference to ᶜUmar is and how successful these stipulations were in producing the desired effect. The jurists' constant reminders of the need to respect them may be a sign that they were not actually adhered to. Moreover, rulers often announced their rejection of them, for example by abolishing certain taxes, as a maneuver to conciliate the populace when the need arose. However, things would soon return to what they were before.[120]

The Muslims' procedure did not significantly differ from that of the followers of other religions after the death of prophets or messengers, when the founders of these religions as institutions—e.g. the dispersed Jews after the Babylonian captivity in the sixth century and the Christian disciples of Paul—created factions sharing a number of characteristics, such as ritual prohibitions and doctrines. The tendency to create such distinct factions gradually emerged among Muslims during the reign of ᶜUmar as a direct result of the expansion of the territory under Islamic power and the spread of Muslims within it. However, it is worth noting that the formation of a Muslim group distinct in its behavior from non-Muslim groups was an urbanite tendency rather than a Bedouin or rural one. This was due to the fact that, on the one hand, the Bedouins adopted Islam, and were introduced to its texts, rites, and rules of conduct later than the urbanites[121] and, on the other hand, that in a Bedouin society

[119] With reference to ᶜUmar b. al-Khattāb.

[120] On this subject, see Abdelmajid Sharfi, *Al-Fikr Al-Islami Fil Rad ᶜAla Al-Nasāra* (Islamic thought in response to Christianity), pp. 183–185.

[121] Al-Tijani says in his account of the journey he made at the beginning

people found it both easier to identify with, and harder to stand out as distinct from, one another. When Islam reached the Bedouins none of them thought of imposing on women obligations such as wearing the veil and being confined to the home, which prevailed in the urban areas. This shows that the will to stand out as distinct has its limits, set primarily by social considerations and the dominant way of life. At the same time, attempts at distinction always take on a religious coloring, which varies in different environments and circumstances, and which always seeks to exclude the other by focusing on what distinguishes peoples and not on what unites them into like-minded groups.

Secondly, institutionalization manifests itself in the transformation of the different forms of worship into unified rituals, which leave no room for personal effort or reasoning (ijtihād) or for any deviation from the established bases or 'pillars' (Arkān). It is well known that rituality is a phenomenon accompanying all religions, whether these rituals be few or many, simple or complicated, periodic (taking place daily, weekly, annually) or occasional (performed at birth, circumcision, marriage, death, or times of crisis, such as droughts), practiced under the supervision of a priest (the rabbi in Judaism, the Immam in Islam) or whoever plays that role in religions lacking an ordained priesthood, or without any supervision. Historical Islam was no exception in this respect, and it was gradually established in the Islamic consciousness that worship through prayer and fasting can only be performed in a specific manner, whether it was obligatory (farḍ), recommended (sunna), or supererogatory (nāfilah,

---

of the eighth century of the hijra: "The people of Ghamrasin (south of Tunisia) are only Muslims by name. They do not know what prayer is, nor do they perform it. We have stayed with them a while and we never heard them call for prayer although they had a place they called the Masjid (Mosque), where only visiting strangers pray. They... do not wash their dead, nor do they allow the daughter a share of her father's inheritance," Tunis, 1958, p. 187.

carried out voluntarily). I have already portrayed the great flexibility that characterizes the Islamic Mission in this respect. However, in due course this flexibility was eliminated altogether and the way in which the Prophet worshiped came to be regarded as obligatory in all its details.

The truth is that these details of worship were not fixed during Mohammed's life, but changed owing to many circumstances, which explains, to some extent, the later disagreements over them between the Imams of the juristic doctrines and their followers. Some of these details were preferred to others and the collective memory retained only those that had gained general consensus, whether the prophet actually performed or was merely thought to have performed them. The Muslims and their scholars would never have agreed on anything had they not been able to imagine a possible alternative, which would maintain the unity of the Islamic nation and save it from divisions. Of the groups that emerged at the time of ᶜAli each strived for a distinctive mark in the performance of its rites, and some of these marks became the cause of many bloody conflicts, such as the Shi'ites' insistence on inserting the phrase "Ḥayya ᶜala Khair al-ᶜamal" (Come to the doing of good) in the call to prayer (Adhān) and the Sunnis' refusal.[122] There was no thought of granting Muslims the freedom to worship in whatever way they considered to be the best, because in the social circumstances of that time diversity was not looked upon as a feature that enriched life or as a universal law of nature manifested in all living things, the opposite of which would only mean death. On the contrary, diversity was something to be feared and guarded against. As a result, formalities and appearances came to rule over the spirit of worship and the sincerity and spontaneity of feeling. Prayer

[122] See, for example, the events that occured concerning the Mosque of Bratha in the fourth and fifth centuries after the hijra: ᶜAbdul Raḥmān Ibn al-Jauzi, *al-Muntathim*, Beirut, 1992, 13–15.

became mere kneeling and prostration at designated times—a set of mechanical motions performed mindlessly, without any awareness of their purpose. Similarly, fasting in most Muslim societies became mere abstinence from food and drink, nothing but a reduction of work and effort by day, while indulging in all kinds of pleasure and cheap entertainment at night. The Ḥajj too turned into a set of prescribed rites practiced in the same manner by all pilgrims, no longer distinguished by the length and distance of the journey or by the dangers and hardships of traveling.

The spread of rituality was one of the major causes of the emergence of Sufism, which began in the third century after the hijra as a marginal movement discontented with the purely superficial religiousness propagated by the jurists, before it was drawn into alliances of all kinds serving a number of practical and symbolic functions, particularly once centralized rule had become weak and the social structure splintered into east and west. The Sufis, who evolved from the Sunni branch of Islam, reacted against the extravagant wealth of the rich and the profligacy and carelessness that usually characterize prosperous societies, such as that of the Abbasids. They also felt that merely performing rituals could not provide them with the spiritual nurture they sought. That is why many of their early protagonists abandoned the performance of rituals, until the majority retreated from this practice, in an attempt to reconcile "shariᶜa" (the law) with "ḥaqīqa" (the truth) and the necessity of respecting al-ẓāhir (the literal, the Appearance) with an appreciation of the depth of al bātin (the esoteric, the Truth). At the same time, they remained generally tolerant towards the various popular forms of worship that involved the mediation and intercession of holy men between God and man. Imagination, bodily expression, and certain collective ritual performances such as reading sections of the Holy Qur'ān ('awrād or 'adhkār), whirling and uttering ecstatic sounds (shaṭaḥāt) were specific to every

Sufi fraternity (tarīqah) and occupied an essential place[123] in their practices.

Thirdly, the institutionalization of religion manifests itself in the formation of a set of fixed dogmas that cannot possibly be refuted. Here it is obvious that the automatic comparison with Christianity does not stand up, because Islam, unlike Christianity, does not entail the necessity of believing in the Trinity, the incarnation, redemption, original sin, and other concepts, all of which are susceptible to a myriad of contradicting exegeses. Nevertheless, in the Islamic sphere too some dogmas arose that fossilized in the course of time and that were more concerned with the requirements of supposedly right conduct than with the content of faith. That is how the Imamate exclusive to ᶜAli and his followers gained a central place in Shi'ite consciousness, being countered by the Sunnis' belief in the precedence of the Rashidun caliphs in managing the Muslims' affairs. However, both the Shi'ites and the Sunnis agreed that the Qur'ān contains "Aḥkām" (judgments, juristic prescriptions) that should be applied literally, regardless of time and place. Little by little, the fundamentalist system, according to which the tradition of the prophet, like the Qur'ān, is a form of revelation (waḥī), came into being. All this resulted in controlling the extraction of law (isṭinbāt) through analogical deduction (qiyās) and presenting the accounts of the prophet's tradition as a "source of knowledge" (jihat ᶜilm). Consequently, it was no longer permissible to slander the chief transmitters of the tradition, who were the companions and close successors of the prophets, even though slandering the inferior groups of transmitters was allowed.

A consideration of Sunni beliefs shows the extent to which Muslims were bound by a set of "dogmas" that were initially controversial. These include the creation of the

[123] See Ira M. Lapidus, "The Institutionalization of Early Islamic Societies," in *Max Weber and Islam*, Toby E. Huff and Wolfgang Schluchter (eds.), New Brunswick, London, 1999, pp. 148–150.

Qur'ān, the belief in predestination (with the consequent denial of man's free will and the plausibility of natural and social phenomena), the arbitrariness of divine judgment, the role of God in life and the afterlife, the sufferings in the tomb and the questions of Munkar and Nakīr,[124] the infallibility of the prophet's companions, and other dogmas thought 'to be necessarily given in religion'. This method of determining what the Muslim should believe only served to establish the solutions proposed by the group that historically gained the upper hand, and to contain the disputes so as to guarantee the continuing authority of the qualified scholars and the representatives of the official religious institutions. It left no room for free thought or for a responsible individual search for answers to existential and metaphysical dilemmas in which no human can claim any absolute and infallible certitude.

The third aspect of the institutionalization of religion may not have been evident at the outset, because the transformation of religion into an institution only comes about gradually and after a period of spontaneous, unprompted religiousness. Moreover, this third aspect required the formation of a group of scholars specializing in matters of religion alone, due to the developments that occurred in Islamic societies as a result of conquests and to the natural tendency towards specialization in a prosperous and diverse civilization. It further required the cooperation of this specialized group with the political authority that had the exclusive right to use violence. No matter how independent holy men may be of politicians, it must be admitted that the contrast between them is a minor one in comparison to the major contrast between those who possess material authority (of a financial or military kind) or moral authority (by virtue of prestige, descent, or knowledge) and those who are deprived

[124] Munkar and Nakīr are the names of two angels who question and if necessary punish the dead in their tombs.

of any authority (the public at large, women, and slaves), even though the latter constitute the majority in every society. The holy men may have been descendants of the mawali (clients) or of the general public, but this did not prevent them from belonging to the elite and enjoying many privileges, once they were acknowledged as such. Thus, they shared with the politicians a relationship of mutual reliance, which became a contentious issue, particularly with the rise of the Abbasid Empire and its use of religious ideology to establish its legitimacy.

I conclude from these three kinds of development that the deviations from the Islamic Mission resulting from institutionalization were not an exception but rather the norm for all religious and non-religious missions. Once the materialization of these missions is attempted in history, the results are always a long way, or at least different, from the original aims. People's opinions, views, and conduct are not subject to prior programming like machines. Nor can they be predicted as in the case of animals governed by instinct alone.[125] People's attitudes change with their circumstances and their psychological and cultural needs, in addition to the imperatives of survival and civilization in general, which in their turn change from one time to another and from one environment to another. It is not unlikely that the increase in the number of Muslims played a role in lowering the standard of religion compared to what it was at the beginning of the mission. For, as much as institutionalized or organized religion tolerates the natural 'popular' tendency towards contentment within the limits that can be controlled and represented in outward behavior and ritual practices, it cannot tolerate any tendencies that may threaten its organization, and it rejects any religious individuality and any attempt to

[125] This fact is stressed by the contemporary philosopher of Greek origins, Castoriadis, in all his writings. Cf. J. F. Bayard, *L'illusion identitaire*, Paris, 1996.

return to the ideal represented by those who first embraced that religion.

In other words, it is wrong to persist in adhering to all the propositions of our predecessors concerning the transition of the Mohammedan Mission from the theoretical level to the practical. They perceived the mission only as far as their historical circumstances allowed, and interpreted it, whether consciously or unconsciously, in accordance with their own interests, intellectual capacities, and the worldly contentions in which they were completely immersed. It is worth noting that the imitation of predecessors and the fear of innovation did not accompany the first applications of Islam but were later phenomena, which came into being as a result of several factors and which reflected a certain balance of power since the victory of the traditionalists over their adversaries, the Muᶜtazilites, at the beginning of al-Mutawakil's caliphate.

The need to examine the appeals to the predecessors critically is proved by the observation that many of the contradictory views ascribed to some of the major figures among them were not always based either on a development in their thought or on the changing course of events, but rather on the fact that in the second century after the hijra, when the Qur'ān was recorded, the halo of saintliness surrounding their names was used to justify the solutions advocated by the jurists and the traditionalists. One of the best two examples is the abundance of narratives about Abu Hurayra in the collections of *Ḥadīth,* although he did not accompany the prophet for more than a few months and his deportment at the time of Muᶜawiya was not exactly exemplary.[126] The second example is the host of accounts—in the books of *tafsīr* (Qur'ānic exegesis), and in particular that by al-Tabari and his successors—of the deeds and views of Abdullah b. ᶜAb-

[126] Sheikh Mahmud Aby Rayya, *Shaykh al-Muḍīra* (the Cairo-Beirut edition) is replete with examples of this.

bas. Although he was interested in knowledge and education, he also participated in the conquests (as one of the seven sons of Abdullah who took part in the first raids on Africa) and politics (in which his behavior, when ᶜAli assigned him to Kufa, was far from honorable). However, as he was only about twelve years old when the Prophet died, he could neither have been a "companion" of the Prophet in the full sense nor a reliable witness to the events of the period of revelation. And yet, who would have dared, in the shadow of the Abbasid state, to challenge the "grandfather of the caliphs" and doubt the soundness of his views?[127]

The institutionalization, which took place gradually after the great changes at the time of the Prophet and directly after, is the form in which Islam has reached us. As a result of the Islamic conquests, the first Muslims had experienced rapid and radical changes in all aspects of life. They came out of their relative isolation in the Arab Peninsula, to interact with peoples and races who adhered to their own beliefs, ethics, habits, traditions and methods of organization. They were unavoidably influenced by the things they saw, and—where these did not contradict the basic principles of the new religion—they added to it a certain Islamic coloring, especially with respect to issues not mentioned in the Qur'ān and to others that had no precedent in the period of revelation. Settling in the conquered regions, marrying their women, and mixing with their people, the Muslims closely examined some civilizations that were more advanced than theirs[128] and ways of life, thought, and expression, that were very different from what they were used to. They adopted

[127] See C. Gilliot, "*Portait mythique d'Ibn ᶜAbbās,*" in *Arabica,* vol. XXXII (1985), pp. 127–184.

[128] In a famous account of ᶜUmar b. al-Khattāb and al-Harmazān after the Islamic invasion of Persia, the occupied say to the occupier: "We thought that you Arabs were in the state of dogs." See, for instance, Mohammad b. Abi Sahl Al- Sarakhsi, *Sharḥ as-Siyar al-Kabīr,* 1/176.

many conceptions, crafts, and functions that go beyond the bare necessities in any civilization, as Ibn Khaldūn explains[129]. Their leaders and nobles moved from hardship and poverty to excessive luxury and wealth. They founded an imperial state and they submitted to a centralized rule in al-Medina, first in Damascus and then in Baghdad, which replaced the authority of the tribal sheikh or existed side by side with it at some times and granted it a degree of jurisdiction at others.

The Islamic system, which was complete or almost complete, could not possibly remain unaffected by these changes. Nevertheless, Muslim consciousness refused to admit this effect, despite its obviousness and depth. That is why the Abbasid theoreticians worked hard to efface it together with all the historical factors that had produced it, while at the same time seeking to prove the continuity between the age of prophecy and the age of stability and institutions. As a result they adhered to the requisites of the Mission not in accordance with their reality, logic, and purpose, but rather in accordance with the outcome of their application after more than a century. In other words, they read the Qur'ān and interpreted the Prophet's life through the perspective and values of their own time and through the conceptual framework that had been formed over more than a century and that employed ready-made stereotypes of thought common to all cultures of the region.[130] Hence the difficulty of my project, which aims to uncover this obscure period and display the wide range of thought in the complete system, so that it may be revealed as it truly was. I intend to

[129] ᶜAbd El-Raḥman Ibn Khaldūn, *The Muqadimmah*, Franz Rosthenthal (Trans.), London, Routledge, 1958, chapter II, "Both Bedouin and sedentary people are natural," 1/249.

[130] As an example, see the use made of the famous account of the spider's web and the cave in which Mohammed and Abū Bakr are reported to have hidden from the polytheists during the hijra.

restore what has been excluded, veiled, and forgotten, and to discover the factors that granted legitimacy to one solution, while denying others, and that made it unlikely for some ideas to occur to Muslims and their scholars in general, although they may have crossed the minds of some unique and outstanding thinkers, without finding a suitable environment in which to surface and crystallize.

For instance, consider the following short quotation from *al-ᶜAmiri's 'Iᶜlam*, in which he discusses the making of jurisprudence: "No matter how strictly individual reasoning is prohibited, there remain only two solutions: either acknowledging the infallible Imam, as the Twelvers (Ithna ᶜAshariyah) claim, or allowing all that *is sanctioned by reason*, as claimed by al-Nazzām. As for the infallible Imam, it would not be possible to locate him and refer to him in every event, and as for resolution on *the basis of what is sanctioned by reason*, this is the gravest heresy to the Hanbalites and the Imamiyya. Thus, it is inevitable that we restore the branches to the roots and adhere to the tradition of the virtuous companions."[131] Al-ᶜAmiri provides no detailed advice on how to dispense with the infallible Imam or how to follow the "tradition of the virtuous companions" and rely on reason alone. Although, unlike the Hanbalites and the Imamiyya, he does not consider the appeal to "what is sanctioned by reason" as a heresy in itself, he does not actually recommend it, because he seeks to unite rather than divide. Nevertheless, his brief allusion to reason shows that some Muslims in the third century saw no need for a religious law—regardless of its source—to govern their social affairs. In other words, they saw no opposition between Islam and the positive law, which made them "secularists" before their time. As a result, their contemporaries failed to recognize the potential hidden

[131] Abu Ḥassan al-ᶜAmiri, *al-'Iᶜlām bi Manāqib al-Islam*, Cairo, 1967, pp. 118–119. (My emphasis)

in their views, which would have opened new horizons, had the Mission not been assigned a legislative role, and had there been a search for the ideal way of harmonizing the different ijtihadat (efforts at reasoning) for the organization of social life: thus they were marginalized and, in due course, forgotten.

Obviously, tracing all the details relating to the period between the Prophet's death and the middle of the second century after the hijra—from which we have only indirect testimonies—and analyzing all the aspects of deviation from the purposes of the Mission is a task beyond the limits of this study. Such a task would require a great deal of original research into the different areas related to Islamic thought before it was recorded in books, treatises, and compilations that have acquired the status of works of reference—Ibn Isḥāq—ibn Hisham's *Sirat*, Ibn Sa^c^d's *al-Tabakāt*, Abu Ḥanīfa's *al-Fiqh al-'Akbar*, Malik's *al-Muwatta'*, al-Shāfi^c^i's treatise *Saḥīḥ al-Bukhāri*, *Saḥīḥ Muslim*, and al Tabari's *Tafsir*[132]—in addition to the works of the Mu^c^tazilites, the Sunnis, and the Shi'ites in jurisprudence, Qur'ānic exegesis, Ḥadīith, and theology, and the works of the Sufis, through which Islam is exclusively studied.

With this in mind, I will focus on the main orientations that have marked the development of Islamic thought and its major countercurrents. I will draw on a number of examples

[132] That is why I do not agree with Mohammad ^c^Abed al-Jabiri who suggests, in his book *Naqd al-^c^Aql al-^c^Arabi*, that the Islamic sciences were created complete. I disagree with that opinion not only because of the great differences that exist between the work of the second- and third-century scholars on the one hand and that of the succeeding centuries on the other, but also because I do not think it right to isolate and overlook the efforts made in the first century and the first half of the second century, just because they have not reached us directly from the writers before the era of recording. The Arab or Islamic mind, if we may refer to it as a singular entity, was formed gradually and it was the first, obscure period of its formation that determined its essential features.

representative of the many different issues in Islamic literature, which cannot be treated summarily without distortion. Bandying texts and juggling with evidence is useless in a work that aims to impart a better understanding of the historical reality, and to avoid the pitfalls of stagnant tribal attitudes and special pleading, which may have a certain psychological or recruitment value, but which do not serve the quest for truth and knowledge.

CHAPTER EIGHT

THEORIZING FOR THE INSTITUTION

Having observed the effects of institutionalization on Islam, I will now examine the traces of this process in the theoretical works of scholars in the different fields of Islamic thought. It is common knowledge that initially these fields were not separate from each other: Qur'ānic exegesis (tafsīr) was not yet an independent science, and neither Ḥadīth nor jurisprudence (fiqh) had definite borders or terms of reference. Similarly, research in scholastic theology was not yet confined to those subjects that would later define that science. The fundamental principles of jurisprudence only came into existence after the establishment of jurisprudence itself, as a means of supplying a framework for the prescribed methods of deduction (istinbāt). All these concerns overlapped and complemented each other, and responded to practical conditions and needs, rather than to the abstract speculations of specialists. The diversity of issues confronting the first Muslims led them to seek momentary solutions to help them define their group and draw its members together. Given the great disparities of race, class, language or dialect, cultural traditions, economic and administrative systems, and interests in general, their desire to overcome their differences and to unify their behavior and their sentiments was quite natural. Since the Mission only touched on a very limited number of issues, and the text—no matter how diverse its exegeses—remained finite while events are infinite, building a harmonious system with religious backing was urgently needed. The Muslims embarked on this project after a great deal of hesitation, vacillation and debate until, in due course, its salient features began to evolve.

In this context I wish to state that the prevalent belief in a similarity between the work of scholars during the era of Qur'ānic recording and the solutions adopted by the predecessors is an illusion, which must be dispelled. The main cause of such a belief is the continuity suggested by the chains of transmission *(salasil as-sanad)* and a dependence on certain accounts in order to defend particular stances, on the assumption that these accounts are impeccable and not susceptible to forgery, distortion, carelessness, and other human flaws. The predecessors and the first generation, particularly in the "naïve phase of religion" (to use the Khaldūnian term), were preoccupied with practical matters above all else. That is why the proposed solutions varied according to the individuals, the circumstances, and the issues involved in each case. It did not occur to anybody that these solutions should be uniform and incorporated into one system, or that they should be referred to a religious authority for acceptance and application.[133]

By emphasizing the necessity of dispelling the illusion in question I am in fact calling for the adoption of Ibn Khaldūn's innovation in his critique of the errors of historians. I will quote at length from his *Muqaddimah*, which provides an excellent introduction to the method used in my own project.[134]

Under "the excellence of historiography and the appreciation of the various approaches to history and a glimpse at the

[133] Unfortunately, there are very few serious studies of this phenomenon, and those that exist—e.g. Abu Sarīᶜ Mohammad ᶜAbd el-Hādī, *Ikhtilāf al-Saḥābah: Asbābuhu wa Āthāruhu fī al-Fiqh al-Islāmī (The Disagreements among the Companions: their Causes and their Effects on Jurisprudence)*, Cairo, 1991—are insufficient in this respect.

[134] ᶜAbd El-Raḥman Ibn Khaldūn, *The Muqadimmah*, Franz Rosthenthal (Trans.), London, Routledge, 1958, 1/15-16, 55-56, 71-76; 2/462.

different kinds of errors to which historians are liable and something about why these errors occur" Ibn Khaldūn states:

"The writing of history requires numerous sources and greatly varied knowledge. It also requires a good speculative mind and thoroughness. The possession of these two qualities leads the historian to the truth and keeps him from slips and error. If he trusts historical information in its plain transmitted form and has no clear knowledge of the principles resulting from custom, the fundamental facts of politics, the nature of civilizations, or the conditions governing human social organization, and if, furthermore, he does not evaluate remote or ancient material through comparison with near or contemporary material, he often cannot avoid stumbling and slipping and deviating from the highroad of truth. Historians, Qur'ān commentators and leading transmitters have committed frequent errors in the stories and events they reported. They accepted them in the plain transmitted form, without regard for its value. They did not check them with the principles underlying such historical situations, nor did they compare them with similar material. Also, they did not probe (more deeply) with the yardstick of philosophy, with the help of the knowledge of things, or with the help of speculation and historical insight. Therefore, they strayed from truth and found themselves lost in the desert of baseless assumptions and errors."

After citing some examples of what he considers as errors and illusions, he adds:

"The scholar in this field needs to know the principles of politics, the true nature of existent things, and the differences among nations, places, and periods with regard to ways of life, character qualities, customs, sects, schools, and everything else. He further needs a comprehensive knowledge of present conditions in all these respects. He must compare similarities or differences between present and past (or distantly located) conditions. He must know the causes of the similarities in certain cases and of the differing origins and the beginning of different dynasties and religious groups, as well as of the reasons and incentives that brought them into being and the circumstances that supported them. His goal must be to have complete knowledge of the reasons for every happening and to be acquainted with the origin of every event. Then he must check transmitted information with the basic principles he knows. Otherwise, the historian must consider it as spurious and dispense with it... A hidden pitfall of historiography is disregard for the fact that conditions within nations and races change with the change of periods and the passing of days. This is a sore affliction and is deeply hidden, becoming noticeable only after a long time, so that rarely do more than a few individuals become aware of it. The condition of the world and of nations, their manners and sects, does not persist in the same form or in a constant manner. There are differences according to days and periods, and changes from one condition to another. This is the case with individuals, times, and cities, and, in the same manner, it happens in connection with regions and districts, periods and dynasties."

At the start of the first book, Ibn Khaldūn lists the causes of lies and errors in the accounts of historians:

"If the soul is impartial in receiving information, it devotes to that information the share of critical investigation the information deserves, and its truth and untruths thus become clear. However, if the soul is inflicted with partisanship for a particular opinion or sect, it accepts without a moment's hesitation the information that is agreeable to it. Prejudice and partisanship obscure the critical faculty and preclude critical investigation.

Reliance upon transmitters.

Unawareness of the purposes of an event.

Unfounded assumption as to the truth of a thing. It results mostly from the reliance upon transmitters.

Ignorance of how conditions conform with reality, due to the fact that they are affected by ambiguities and artificial distortions.

The fact that people as a rule approach great and high-ranking persons with praise and encomiums. They embellish conditions and spread the fame (of great men). The information made public in such cases is not truthful.

Another reason for making untruth unavoidable is ignorance of the natures of various conditions arising in civilization. Every event (or phenomenon) whether (it comes into being in connection with some) essence or (as a result of an) action, must inevitably possess a nature peculiar to its essence as well as to the accidental conditions that may attach themselves to it. If the student knows the nature of events and the circumstances and requirements in the world of existence, it will help him distinguish truth from untruth in investigating the historical truth critically. This is more effective in critical investigation ... and superior to the investigations that rely upon criticism of the personalities of transmitters. Such personality criticism should not be resorted to until it has been ascertained whether a specific piece of information is in itself possible, or not. If it is absurd, there is no use engaging in personality criticism."

This sounds as if it had been written yesterday and not about six centuries ago. It shows no signs of being outmoded, and but for some stylistic peculiarities one could easily ascribe it to a contemporary writer. However, Ibn Khaldūn was precluded by a psychological and social barrier from applying his method to accounts relating to the science of religion, and thus he states immediately after his list of the causes of untruth:

"Personality criticism is taken into consideration only in connection with the soundness (or lack of soundness) of

Muslim religious information, because this religious information mostly concerns injunctions in accordance with which the Lawgiver (Mohammed) enjoined Muslims to act whenever it can be presumed that the information is genuine, the way to achieve presumptive soundness is to ascertain the probity (ᶜadālah) and exactness of the transmitters."

He then summarizes his opinion at the end of the chapter on the science of Ḥādīth as follows: "Of all people, scholars most deserve that one have a good opinion of them and that one be eager to find excuses for them."

If this is true, the time has come to overcome the barrier that forced Ibn Khaldūn to distort the truth by describing "Muslim religious information" as "mostly injunctions," whereas a glance at any monograph of jurisprudence, Qur'ānic exegesis or Ḥādīth from the second or third century after the hijra—which form the basis of jurisprudential prescriptions or judgments (Aḥkām)—suffices to prove the falsity of such an opinion. In fact all these "injunctions" (*takālīf*) occur in transmitted accounts (isnād), which can sometimes be traced back to the Prophet, but which most of the time stop at the level of the companions, the successors, and particularly the Imams of the sects. Thus, it is impossible to distinguish, in these accounts, between figurative tropes (inshā') and historical information.[135] Ibn Khaldūn was led into this error precisely by what he criticized at a theoretical level when dealing with non-religious issues, that is, "partisanship for a particular opinion or sect," "reliance upon transmitters," and "ignorance of the various conditions arising in civilization" in the Khaldūnian sense, which includes all man's social institutions, crafts and sciences. What is at issue here is not the presence or absence of sound speculation, but rather the flaws inherent in any kind of in-

[135] See Hunayda Ḥafsa, *Ḥuḍur an-Naṣṣ al-Qur'ani fil-Mudawanna al-Kubra* (The Presence of the Qur'ānic Text in the Grand Record), submitted for the DRA degree, Humanities Department, Manuba, 1999.

formation, and the illusions, forgetfulness, errors, and slips that afflict the transmitter, no matter how hard he tries to be honest, precise, and accurate in transmitting what he has heard. Nowadays, no historian deserving the title will rely, in his search for knowledge of the present and the past, on such methods of transmission, regardless of how truthful, qualified, pious, and impartial the transmitters are said to be.

The historian no longer claims to have absolute knowledge of the truth. Events have no single, objective existence but rather acquire their meaning from the way people view them, each according to his or her perspective, qualifications and circumstances. The historian, therefore, creates the past as much as he conveys it. If he is aware of the limitations of his knowledge, he will not only be critical of the information transmitted to him but also very alert to the various material and intellectual factors that may motivate the different interpretations of the events he is analyzing. A sound method dictates that the historian, without falling victim to relativism, should carefully observe the internal harmony of events, rather than project onto them his personal interests or the interests of his contemporaries and ascribe to a certain historical condition something that may only apply to another, completely different one. From this point of view, historicizing the first century after the hijra requires a reconsideration of various postulates, and particularly those relating to the faithfulness of the first Muslim generation to the principles of the Mission—the very principles they were called upon to substantiate in reality.

I will not repeat what I have already said about the characteristics of the Prophet's behavior when faced with the responsibility for fostering the Islamic nation at its embryonic stage in Mecca and later on at its infant stage in Madina. I will only emphasize the flexibility that characterized this behavior. Mohammed intended to raise the Muslim generations on new values, which were in many ways incompatible with the ways of the people before Islam. However, from time to time he took account of the traditional ways by adopting a realistic and gradual approach and by prioritizing those things that seemed more important, given the requirements of the time and the balance of power.[136] Arbitrating in disputes seems to have been one of the most important tasks undertaken by Mohammed in this domain. He carried out this task himself in those cases which were referred to him personally, while in distant regions, such as Yemen, he entrusted it to a number of his companions. When the Prophet died, the Caliphs acted as arbitrators at the center of the Empire, and appointed judges in the conquered regions. Thus, the inevitable happened. The institution of arbitration known in the tribal system was largely replaced by the judicial authority that was closely tied to the new centralized rule. The judge no longer derived his authority from the consent of the disputing parties, as had the arbitrator, but from the political authority that appointed and provided him with the power to execute his judgments.

These judges neither received any special training nor referred to a "legal code," such as that decreed by Justinian for the Byzantine Empire in the sixth century. They had some knowledge of the precedents adjudicated by Mohammed and alluded to in the waḥī, but this related more to the circumstances surrounding the incidents in question than to the resulting judgments, since many of them had not personally witnessed the procedures. The cases that were brought before them were doubtless more varied and complex than the precedents, and often concerned social and economic problems that bore no relation to the era of the Prophet. Moreover, they involved people who did not have the same morals, habits, traditions, and lifestyles as the Arabs in Ḥijāz and in the Peninsula in general. The inhabitants of Iraq, Persia, and

[136] The best example of this is the Prophet's assent—despite his own views on women—to ᶜUmar's insistence on commanding them to wear the veil and beating them, in adherence to the customs of the Quraysh rather than those of the people of the Madina.

Egypt had inherited highly sophisticated civilizations and ruling systems, and life in the valleys of the great rivers (Nile, Tigris, and Euphrates), with its wide-ranging agricultural activities, was very different from that in the arid desert regions. All this had an influence on the nature of social relations, on the way people viewed the role of centralized power and its representatives, and on the image of the judge, the men responsible for collecting taxes, and others who performed different state functions.

Quite properly, these Muslim judges tried to apply the conventions they had known in their Arab environment, while adapting to, and confirming, many of the customs prevalent among the natives of the conquered regions, if these customs did not essentially contradict the principles of Islam. However, some, for practical purposes, may have gone further than that and sought to learn about the legal rules that had been in existence in the conquered regions beforehand, in particular with respect to administration and the collection of taxes. Thus, they acquired knowledge of the ways of the Romans, the Persians, the Jews, and others, which goes some way to explain the resemblance between the Islamic legal system on the one hand and the laws in force in the Mediterranean[137] on the other. In the absence of elaborate texts and recorded standards, it was only natural that the judgments pronounced by judges differed from one place to another according to differences in the mood, character, and circumstances of the individuals. This lack of consistency was a source of anxiety for both the judges and the judged, particularly since the matters under judgment were not only minor disputes but also issues of blood, honor, and other vital interests, as well as the validity or otherwise of various rituals.

[137] On this subject, see Jeanne Ladjili, *Histoire jurisdique de la Mediterranée: droit romain, droit musulman*, Tinus, 1990.

JURISPRUDENCE

The inconsistencies in judgments left permanent marks on jurisprudence, despite the jurists' efforts to resolve the contradictions and to create some kind of harmony between procedures in the different parts of the Islamic world. These attempts at constructing a consistent system concurred with the logic of the emerging Empire, which required that the Muslims, as a community destined to spread and embrace many different individuals and groups, should have a unified system of worship (ᶜibadāt) and administration (muᶜamalāt). To achieve this difficult aim, scholars in every region—particularly Ḥijāz, Syria, and Iraq—sought to establish the validity of their choices and to justify them by the best possible means. They did so by using traditional accounts in support of any one solution that they favored over all others.

This observation may help to explain the controversy between *Ahl al Ra'y* (appliers of reason) and the *Muḥadithūn* (traditionalists), which began in the second century after the hijra and intensified in the third, with the emergence of the Imams, whose views were adopted and championed by their disciples. In contrast, during the period immediately following the prophet's death and throughout the first century only personal opinion and free reasoning (ijtihād) had been resorted to, without any reference to the Qur'ānic text or to Mohammed's deeds and his sayings about any matter, whether trivial or grave, and without any comparisons between the present and the past or between the "branches" (positive law) and the "roots" (the theoretical basis of the law). That is probably the main reason why Islamic jurisprudence, even after being recorded and codified, remained a compendium of individual cases, which were subsequently categorized in books and chapters, but which is very hard, if not impossible, to subordinate to general principles that may throw light on their particular details, as is normally the case with legal records. Despite its profuseness, Islamic jurisprudence lacks a detailed account of causes and purposes.

Rather than constructing a legislative system in the technical sense of the term, it fostered modes of interaction based on trust, in a moral rather than legal sense, and on the threat of financial sanctions, which in fact contradicted the notion of contracting and abiding by the conditions of a contract.

One must not be deceived by one school's acceptance of some elements of 'usul (the theoretical basis of Islamic law), such as consensus (ijma[c]) and analogical deduction (qiyās), and another school's denial of them, as is the case, for example, with the Hanafite and al-Zahiri or the Ja[c]farai Hanbalite schools, because the disagreements concern not so much the solutions adopted by each school as the justification of those solutions. If one considers the *Mudawana* of Saḥnoun al-Maliki, the *Muḥalā* of Hazm al-Zahiri, or indeed *al-Da[c]ā'm* by the judge al-Nu[c]man al-Isma[c]ili, one finds many differences in the validation of judgments (Mustanadāt al Aḥkām). Thus one may come across references to the authority of Shi'ite Imams or to Aḥād traditions, with a reliance on the views of Malik and Ibn al-Qassim that prevailed in Medina, in the former case. However, these discrepancies are no greater than those between al-Shāfi[c]i's *Umm* and al-Shibani al-Ḥanafi's *Mabsout* or Ibn Qudamah al-Ḥanbāli's *Mughni*. The jurisprudential works of the schools retained a large number of conflicting solutions that characterized the early phases of Islam. The Islamic coloring added to these judgments remained transparent and could not hide the fact that they were mere subterfuges or unfounded assertions, reflecting the historical and cultural conditions in which they were made.

Arab readers are probably aware that Malik rejected Caliph al-Mansour's offer to declare his *Muwatta'* an official work sanctioned by the Abbasid political and judicial authorities. They may also know about the famous dispute between Caliph al-Ma'mūn and al-Majusi, in which the Caliph praised the fact that the disagreements among Muslims concerned only the branches and not the roots. He saw this as a broadening of possibilities rather than as a diminution of the validity and consistency of the Muslims' religion and beliefs. There are many books on the disagreements of jurists, the most renowned being probably Ibn Rushd's *Bidayat al-Mujtahad wa Nihayat al-Muqtasad* and al-Dimashqi al-Shāfiᶜi's *Raḥmat al-Umma fī Ikhtilāf al 'A'ima*—written, respectively, in the sixth and the eighth century after the hijra[138]—and work on the subject continues to the present day, as shown, for instance, by al-Jaziri's *al-Fiqh ᶜala al-Mazahib al-Arbaᶜa.*

In addition to the Hanfites' "ploys" to avoid the passing of judgments, the debates on the legitimacy or otherwise of "fabrication" (i.e. choosing from the judgments of four different schools) and the numerous contemporary attempts at mediation between the schools, many conferences and symposia have been held on this subject, but without any significant results so far. The general opinion is that, no matter how severe the disagreements of jurists, jurisprudence contains "God's judgments" or the "judgment of the sharᶜ" in all cases.[139] This may sound incompatible with the simplest intuitive facts. Nevertheless it is constantly emphasized that whatever has been decreed by the jurists of the different schools and their disciples is no human legislation, for God is the only legislator. Supposedly, the decrees are always true and there is no harm in the inconsistencies they may contain. These two postulates require more reflection on my part.

To avoid a merely theoretical discussion, I will cite from al-Dimashqi's book some examples of the issues on which

[138] Of the former see, for instance, the two-volume edition, published in Cairo in 1996, of the latter the second edition, published in Cairo in 1967.

[139] It may be worth noting that in this respect there was no essential difference between Muslim and Christian jurists: the former speak of "God's sharᶜ" and the latter of "God's nāmūs" (both meaning the law of God). See Stefan Leder, *Das Vierte Buch der Kanons der Könige aus der Sammlung des Makerios,* Frankfurt am Main, 1985, p. 30. Many of the "laws" mentioned in this book are very similar to the judgements of Islamic jurists.

the jurists reached a "consensus," and some others, on which they disagreed. I will examine the extent of their validity and their fidelity to divine law, recalling my earlier comments on the purposes of the Mohammedan Mission.

- Malik and al-Shāfiᶜi find it permissible for a man to pray beside a woman, whereas Abu Ḥanīfa says that in this event the man's prayer is void.
- Where a road or a river separates the Imam (the prayer leader) from the Ma'mūm (the followers in prayer), the 'I'timam (the leading of prayer) is valid according to al-Shāfiᶜi, and not valid according to Abu Ḥanīfa. If a follower prays in his own house and the Imam in the Mosque and there is a barrier between them, Malik, al-Shāfiᶜi, and Ahmad argue that the prayer is not valid, whereas Abu Ḥanīfa argues that it is.
- All four agree that praying for the dead requires purity (ablution) and the covering of the private parts. However, Ash-Shaᶜbi and Mohammed b. Jarīr al-Tabari dispense with the requirement of ablution.
- There is broad agreement that suicides should be prayed for, but al-Uzaᶜi, for one, dissents. In Qutāda's view, no prayers should be said for an illegitimate child, and in al-Ḥasan's, for a woman during the period of her seclusion after childbirth.
- According to al-Shāfiᶜi, Malik, and Abu Ḥanīfa, a man who undertakes a journey after beginning the day fasting must not break his fast, whereas Ahmad b. Ḥanbāl, and al-Muzni after him, believes that it is permissible for him to do so.
- The al-ᶜAqīqa sacrifice is a recommended sunna (tradition) according to Malik and al-Shāfiᶜi. Abu Ḥanīfa states that "it is permissible but I do not say recommended." Concerning Ahmad, two accounts are available: according to one, he recommended the sacrifice, according to the other he regarded it as obligatory, and some of his companions opted for the latter. Generally, two ewes were supposed to be

sacrificed for a new baby boy, and one for a baby girl, but Malik stipulates one for either sex.

- As to whether or not the house and the indispensable servant of an insolvent person should be sold, Abu Ḥanīfa and Ahmad state that they should not be sold, and Abu Ḥanīfa extends this prohibition to his entire estate or property. On the other hand, Malik and al-Shāfiᶜi rule that everything should be sold.

- The lawfulness of al-Musāqāt[140] is asserted by the jurists among the Prophet's companions and successors, and the Imams of the schools, with the only opposing voice being that of Abu Ḥanīfa.

- There is disagreement as to whether or not blood relatives who are not assigned a share in an estate by the Qur'ān may inherit. There are ten categories of such blood relatives, including the father of the mother, the grandchildren of the daughter, the nieces of the brother, the nephews of the sister, maternal nephews, female cousins, maternal aunts, and some others. Malik and al-Shāfiᶜi believe that these should not inherit and the money should go to charity, as do Abū Bakr, ᶜUmar, ᶜUthman, Zayd, al-Zahri, al-Uzaᶜi, and Daoud. On the other hand, Abu Ḥanīfa and Ahmad believe that they should inherit, and the same is also reported of ᶜAli, Ibn Masᶜud, and Ibn ᶜAbbas. In the absence of any blood relative belonging to the ten categories, the nearest male relatives (ᶜAsabāt) are said to be entitled to certain prescribed quotas (Furūḍ).

- Marriage, for al-Shāfiᶜi and Ahmad, is lawful only if it is contracted in the presence of a male guardian. It is not permissible for a woman to give herself in marriage. Abu Ḥanīfa

[140] Musaqat: a legal term denoting the lease of a plantation for one crop period with profit-sharing. The contract for such a lease is between the owner of the plantation and the husbandman (ᶜāmil), who undertakes to tend the trees or vines of the plantation for one season, at the end of which the proceeds of the crop are divided between the two parties. (*Encyclopedia of Islam*)

allows a woman to represent herself or appoint a guardian if she is entitled to dispose of her own money, unless she is trying to marry a man beneath her, in which case the guardian may object. Malik lays down that if she is honorable, beautiful and desirable she can only be married through a guardian, but if she is not, a stranger may give her in marriage with her consent.

- Generally, marriage is only deemed lawful with three witnesses, but Malik, Abu Ḥanīfa, al-Shāfiᶜi, and Ahmad grant the parties some discretion in this respect.

- The power over divorce should belong to the man in the opinion of Malik, to the woman in that of Abu Ḥanīfa.

- There is general agreement that the minimum period of pregnancy is six months, but none as to the maximum. Abu Ḥanīfa speaks of two years, and Malik is reported to have suggested four, five and seven years. Al-Shāfiᶜi's choice is four years. Ahmad shares al-Shāfiᶜi's view, according to the best-known account, and Abu Ḥanīfa's, according to another.

- If one man holds down another, who is killed by a third, Abu Ḥanīfa and Al-Shāfiᶜi regard the man who kills, and not the man who holds the victim, as punishable, while Malik claims that both are accomplices and deserve punishment, if the killer could not have carried out his deed without the assistance of the holder. Ahmad declares in one account that the killer should be killed and the holder imprisoned for life, and in another that both should be killed.

- It is generally agreed that any blood-money required to be paid by a free Muslim woman should be half of that required of a free Muslim man. However, there is disagreement as to whether or not her offenses (jirāḥ) equal his.

- All the Imams deem the blood-money for accidental killing to be the responsibility of the killer's ᶜAqila (the group of people sharing liability with the killer), deferred for three years. They disagree as to whether the killer should pay a share of the blood-money and whether the payment required of the ᶜAqila should be predetermined or assessed in accordance with the ᶜAqila's capabilities.

- As a penalty for drinking wine, Abu Ḥanīfa and Malik prescribe eighty lashes, and al-Shāfiᶜi forty, while Ahmad opts for eighty according to one account, and forty according to another. Abu Ḥanīfa, Malik and Ahmad agree that the penalty should be exacted by means of a whip, while al-Shāfiᶜi stipulates the use of the hem of a robe, hands, or shoes.

- As to whether it is lawful for a woman to be a judge, Malik and al-Shāfiᶜi rule that it is not. According to Abu Ḥanīfa it is lawful for her to pass judgment on all matters in which the testimony of a woman is accepted, that is, everything except offenses and penalties. Ibn Jarīr al-Tabari allows her to be a judge in all matters, without exception.

From these observations I draw the following conclusions:

1. All the cases I have cited lack clear Qur'ānic textual references, even if the text is sometimes brought into play through analogical deduction or specific exegesis. A number of them contain conflicting traditions, some of which go back to the Prophet and others only to his companions, having probably been composed at a later time in support of solutions sanctioned by the Imams of the schools.

2. All these cases relate to ᶜibadat (ritual and worship) as well as muᶜamalat (administration and legal obligations). Where the standardizing and unifying of rituals (ᶜibadāt) occurred in response to the requirements of worldly administration (muᶜamalāt), the bestowal of sanctity on the latter in a specific historical situation greatly hampered the development of Islamic societies, particularly when conditions changed and the need for a new basis of interaction arose.

3. The consequences of these disparities are not always minor ones. They sometimes affect the validity of a ritual—for example, in relation to a man praying next to a woman, or to fasting on journeys—or the lawfulness of marriages (Furrūj) with or without the presence of a guardian and wit-

nesses. They may even extend to matters of life and death, as in the issue of the penalty for the accomplice of a murderer.[141]

4. It is evident that the agreements and disagreements between jurists correspond to the values prevalent at the time of the emergence of jurisprudence in Islamic societies, which shared some features and not others. For example, their consensus about the inequality between men and women concerning the diyya (blood-money) was determined by their views on women in general. However, the fact that Abu Ḥanīfa's grants women the right to divorce, and al-Tabari' the right to pass judgment on all matters, indicates that—despite the common view of women as inferior—the status of Iraqi women in some social classes was different from that of their Ḥijazi or Egyptian sisters.

5. The jurists' agreements and disagreements clearly reflect the tribal customs and rituals in the Arab Peninsula. This is demonstrated by their views on the collective responsibility of the tribe when one of its members has committed an offense, and on the practice of ᶜAqīqa. They also reveal the standard of knowledge at the time, for instance in connection with the determination of the maximum period of pregnancy and even with the question of prayers for women after childbirth.

6. Last but not least, the inconsistencies of the jurists show that in decreeing their judgments the jurists made concessions to conflicting economic interests. This led them to disagree on the issues of inheritance by blood relatives, the judgment of Musāqāt (partnership with respect to trees), and

[141] That is why Abu Ḥayān al-Tawḥīdī complains: "What is it that allows some jurists to talk of the lawfulness of a farj (marriage) while others speak of its unlawfulness? Similarly, with respect to money and life, one jurist decrees the death penalty while another forbids it. They woefully disagree with each other, hideously manipulate the people, and follow their lusts and desires," Abu Ḥayān al-Tawḥīdī, *al-Hawāmil wa ash-Shawāmil*, Cairo, 1951, paragraph 153.

the sale of the possessions—in particular the house—of an insolvent person.

If we overlook the particular agreements and disagreements between the jurists, and examine their views in general, we arrive at the following characteristics:

First, they were more concerned with external rituals of worship and legal obligations than with the development of an internal personal morality that would direct Muslims towards good and away from evil. That is why they raised the imperatives of community above individual responsibility, focusing on duties at the expense of rights, although it could hardly have been otherwise when there were so many different views of Muslims' religious obligations (taklīf). The jurists appointed themselves speakers in God's name and claimed exclusive knowledge of what He desires, commands, rejects, and forbids. They believed that "those whom God does not wish to understand his purposes are not obliged to do so." They went so far as to suggest that, even in the most feminine matters such as menstruation, God wanted women to follow the legal advice of the Mufti. God did not oblige women to comprehend, or listen to, accounts of menstruation, let alone the "detailing of the generalities and particularities of their gender.[142] Such views were obviously a result of the division of labor, which was, in its turn, a consequence of certain economic conditions and bore no relation whatsoever to divine will.

In accordance with the rule that every act of disqualification provokes an equal, or even more powerful, act of counter-disqualification, the followers of the Sunna, the

[142] Fakhreddin Al-Rāzī, *al-Mahsūl*, 3/220–221. This disparity in obligations reflects a discriminating view that denies the other's humanity in general (whether the difference is one of sex, color, etc.). For instance, consider Ibn al-Riwandi's criticism of al-Muᶜtazilah's claim that "negroes can in fact write poetry and treatises," *Fadiḥat al-Muᶜtazilah (The scandal of the Muᶜtazilah)*, Beirut/Paris, 1975–1977, p. 131.

Khawarij, and the Shi'ites, whether moderate or fanatical, regarded themselves as being fitter to know the truth than the followers of the opposite schools. A well-known example is Sahnun, the African Maliki leader, who tried to expel the Hanafites from the study circles in the Qayrawan Mosque. A similar situation existed until recently in those Islamic countries where there were several schools of jurisprudence or many different groups competing for legitimacy and popularity. Delivering legal opinions (fatāwa) was a weapon used by the various factions, to such an extent that a new term, "tafati" (to bandy fatāwas), was coined in the Arabic language. The mystical Sufis scorned the jurists who looked down on the common people, calling them "the scholars of evil" and likening them to "the rock which blocks the mouth of the river, and neither drinks nor lets the water reach the plants."[143] The rationalist philosophers saw themselves as better suited to understand and interpret religion than the theologians and exegetes.[144] And so on.

[143] Abu Tālib al-Maccī, *Qūt al-Qulūb*, Cairo, 1991, vol. 2, p. 97. See the whole chapter devoted to the discussion of the differences between the worldly scholars and those who believed in the afterlife, and the disparagement of "the scholars of evil," pp. 94–104. Al-Ghazali's stance in *Jawahir al-Qur'ān*, Beirut, 1977, is not very far from that of Abu Tālib al-Maccī.

[144] It is interesting that Ibn Rushd (Averroës) justifies the distinction he makes between the "demonstrative class" and the other classes by a specific interpretation of the seventh verse of the chapter on the family of ᶜUmran: "He it is who has revealed the Book to you: some of its verses are decisive, they are the basis of the Book, and others are allegorical: then as for those in whose hearts there is perversity, they follow the part of it which is allegorical, seeking to mislead, and seeking to give it their own interpretation, but none knows its interpretation except Allah, and those who are firmly rooted in knowledge say: We believe in it, it is all from our Lord, and none do mind except those having understanding" (Aal ᶜUmran 7/3). In response to al-Ghazāli, who accuses philosophers of heresy (in respect of the pre-eternity of the word, God's ignorance of particulars, and the resurrection the body in the next life) he writes: "These are allegorical interpretations which ought not to be expressed except to those who are qualified to receive allegories. These are 'those who are well-grounded in

Second, the rise of a specific category of scholars who claimed the exclusive right to deal with the sacred led many others to stray from their initial task towards a contemptible behavior that caused al-Kindī to describe the holy men of his time as being "estranged from the truth, even if they were crowned with the crowns of the truth, which they do not deserve ... They defend the positions they have falsely gained, in order to establish their leadership and to trade in religion. They lack religion, because he who trades in something sells it, and he who sells something no longer owns it. Thus, he who trades in religion has no religion and it is just and lawful that he who denies the knowledge of things in their essence and calls such knowledge blasphemy be stripped of religion."[145] Abu al-Hassan al-ᶜĀmiri stresses this deviation by pointing out its symptoms: "When the jurists turned their noble craft, which should aim at the good of the two territories of Islam, into an instrument for controlling the people, gaining the favor of Sultans, acquiring the property of the weak, and nullifying rights by base means, this craft turned from one deserving praise into one inviting contempt."[146] There are many examples of this, since it is difficult to oppose people who claim to be speaking in the name

---

knowledge'." In connection with his classification of people into the "rhetorical class" (which includes the majority of the public), the "dialectical class" (the theologians), and the "demonstrative class" (the philosophers), he states with reference to the same verse: "With regard to the apparent texts ... when there is a self-evident doubt whether it is apparent to everyone and whether knowledge of its interpretation is impossible to them, they should be told that it is ambiguous and its meaning known by no one except God; and that the stop should be put here in the sentence of the Exalted: 'And no one knows the interpretation thereof except Allah'" Ibn Rushd, *Kitāb Faṣl al-Maqāl (The Decisive Treatise)*, George F. Hourani (trans.), London, 1961, p. 53, 66. On this subject cf. Abdelmajid Sharfi, "Fi Thikra Abi al-Walid" (In Memory of Abu Walid [Ibn Rushd]), *Riḥab al-Maᶜrifah* (Tunis), no. 3, May–June 1998, pp. 18–22.

[145] "Kitab al-Kindī ila al-Muᶜ tasim billa fi al-Falsafa al-'ūla" in Al-Kindī, *Rasā'il al kindi al falsāfia,* (Al Kindi's Philosophical Treatise).

[146] Abu Ḥassan al-ᶜĀmiri, *al-'Iᶜlām bi Manaqib al-Islam*, p. 154.

of God, when they form a solid group to defend their own interests, particularly in the absence of any effective counter-authorities, as in the case of the ancient Muslim—or non-Muslim—societies.

Third, the jurists' aspiration to emulate the forefathers led to forms of behavior that bore no original relation to religion, but were forcibly introduced into Islamic literature. The following example of the feebleness of that stance may serve as one of many: "ᶜAiād relates of Malik, may God be pleased with him, that he visited ᶜAbdullah b. Sālih, Prince of Medina. He sat for an hour, then the Prince called for ablution (wudu') and food, and said: 'Start with Abu ᶜAbdullah'. Malik said (meaning himself): 'Abu Abdullah does not wash his hands, because that is not what the scholars of our country have laid down, but a foreign custom. When ᶜUmar ate he used to wipe his hands on the soles of his feet... Quit the tradition of the foreigners and revive that of the Arabs'."[147] Imitation—together with many other factors—also led to a refusal to take into consideration and analyze any natural causes. This way of thinking immediately turns to the first cause, as it does, for example in relation to diseases, excluding the role of medicine and threatening those who resort to it with severe pain, as in the famous lines by one of the Andalusian poets during the reign of Bani Nasr:

[147] Ahmad b. Yehya (al-Talmisani) al-Wanasharisi, *al-Miᶜyār*, Beirut, 1981, 2/508. It is important to note here that some jurists did not approve of imitation in all cases. Ibn Rushd (the elder): "God has created all people and He has made them into peoples and tribes, each with their specific country, characteristics, and ways. None of them should abandon their chosen ways and customs for those of others, for this difference between God's servants is permissible" *al-Fatawa*, Beirut, 1987, 2/964. Al-Shāṭibi: "If they consider all changes in customs as innovations, then they must consider all forms of food, drink, clothing, and speech that are foreign to them as innovations. This is preposterous, for habits and customs change with time and place. It would make all those who do not imitate the Arab contemporaries of the companions deviants. It is very reprehensible," *al-Iᶜtisām*, Beirut, 1988, 2/77-78.

He who admits that medicine can cure the ill
Has 'gained' himself painful suffering.
Discard all that you see
And rely on Allah the Mighty and the Knowing.[148]

This is hardly surprising, if we bear in mind that, ever since the beginning of imitation, theorists had been trying to promote ignorance and thwart the desire for knowledge, to such an extent that one of them in the Hafsian era declared:

All sciences save the Qur'ān are heresies
With the exception of the ḥadīth and jurisprudence
The source of knowledge is what was transmitted
And everything else is the whispering of devils[149]

Fourth, the most dangerous consequence of the jurists' practices was the Muslims' gradual failure to deal with the Qur'ān in a humane spirit, and the ascendancy of secondary texts that claim to be derived from it. These secondary texts became an obstacle in the way of personal reasoning and open-minded reflection, which ought to take place in an atmosphere of freedom rather than coercion and authoritarianism. The image of the Prophet was blown out of all proportion and endowed with idealistic features, which distanced him from ordinary humans and aligned him with the angels and other imaginary creatures. The Imams of the schools came to be seen by Muslims as infallible, so that no one dared criticize their views or point out any traces in them of the specific historical conditions that had unavoidably contributed to shape them.

[148] Cf. ᶜAbd el-Hamid al-Haramah, *al-Qasida al-Andalusia khilal al-Qarn al-thamin al-HIjri (The Andalusian Poem in the Eighth Century after the Hijra)*, Tripoli, 1996, 1/279.

[149] Cf. Ibrāhim Jadlah, "Manzilat ash-Shiᶜr al-ᶜArabi fi Fikr Ibn Khaldūn," in *al-Masār,* no. 15, March 1993, p. 112, quoted from Ibn Mariym, *al-Bustān,* Algiers, 1908, p. 310.

Finally, this jurisprudence was guilty of two glaring omissions.[150]

First, there were no regulations for the ownership of land. The relevant literature only reiterates the general principle that the land is the property of whoever cultivates it, in addition to some considerations concerning boundaries and irrigation, *waqf* (common possession), *shufʿa* (the right of the co-owner to buy out his partner's share if it is for sale), *fay'* (land considered to belong to the whole Muslim community), and *ghanīmah* (land won as booty). Initially, most agricultural land was collectively owned by the tribe, with the sole exception of the lands set aside by the state for those whom the Sultan wished to reward for certain services. The individuals concerned exploited the farmers and forced them to pay taxes. The farmers, in their turn, were not encouraged by the restrictions on private property to settle down and cultivate the land or invest in it in the long run. Thus, the promulgation of land laws in the Ottoman Empire in 1858, which legitimized land ownership, represented a radical change. The gap that had marked jurisprudence in this respect was closed, and many laws governing the organization of property followed in the different Muslim regions, all of them derived in various ways from western legislations.[151] The delay of jurisprudence in fulfilling its role in this respect resulted in poor agricultural conditions throughout Islamic history, which in turn gave rise to monopolies, high prices, riots, disturbances, famines, and diseases. It was also responsible for enabling the tribal sheikhs in the country and

[150] Of course I refer only to phenomena that existed in the old days but were overlooked by the jurists. The absence of phenomena such as transportation by aircraft or automobile, genetic engineering, electronic trade, and many others that are continually being produced by modern civilization, is only natural and the jurists cannot be blamed for overlooking them.

[151] See W. Warwick, *The Modernization of Administration in the Near East*, Beirut and London, 1963, pp. 59–62.

the rich merchants in the cities to benefit from the modern laws and acquire fortunes at the expense of the people at large, in particular the small farmers who had previously owned the land collectively without any official documents.

Second, the political dimension was missing. During the first four centuries after the hijra, the jurists paid little attention to the organization of this central aspect of social life. They did not attempt to regulate the work of state institutions, but only called for obedience to the ruler, regardless of the means by which he came to power or the manner in which he directed his affairs. Afraid to innovate and to pass judgments without precedents, they failed to catch up with the changes that demanded, alongside the "religious law," new institutions, such as Wilayat al-Mazalim (the structure through which the temporal authority takes direct responsibility for dispensing justice), ḥisba (state intervention in the interests of public morality) and civil courts, as they have come into being in modern times. The jurists' delay also provided the theologians with the opportunity to try and fill the gap by focusing on the Imamate, and gave the rulers a free hand to treat their subjects as they wished, guided by their own desires and interests and only rarely obeying the imperatives of reason, justice, and fairness. When political jurisprudence made its first appearance in the fifth century after the hijra with al-Mawardi's *Aḥkām as-Sultaniyya*, it aimed primarily at justifying the past and underpinning contemporary practices that were characterized by despotism, oppression, and selfishness, rather than by the desire to build a rational system on Qur'ānic principles. The jurists did not understand the prophet's wisdom in demanding that one brother should support the other, even if the latter were a tyrant, because this would persuade him to abandon his tyranny. Nor did they appreciate the prophet's vision of the ruler as guardian and protector in accordance with his redefinition of the role of guardianship, which he rid of its ancient connotations by declaring that "each of you is a guardian." Instead, the jurists followed the admired model of the Chosroes, putting their theories at the service of the rulers' pursuit of power without accountability, and being granted, in return, the right to dictate the forms of social life and to impose unity on all Muslim groups and individuals through stereotyped rituals.

'USUL AL-FIQH

'Usul al-Fiqh (legal theory) might have been expected to perform the task of theorizing, which jurisprudence failed to do as a result of its exclusive concern with positive legal rulings (*furu*ᶜ). However, this art did not come into being until later, when legal thinkers tried to clarify the existing situation by developing theories for the methods of deduction (istinbāt), on the one hand, and providing justifications for the solutions proposed by the first generations, on the other. By holding the inconsistencies that marked the judgments of Caliphs, judges and jurists for about two centuries within bounds, these thinkers managed to contain their negative impact on the integrity of legal judgments, but at the same time prevented the formation of "another" jurisprudence, or a system of rights that would have sought to establish both justice and order on a different basis. A vague desire to bestow an Islamic coloring on the solutions for real or hypothetical problems was already present in people's minds before the end of the second century, but the credit for uncovering it and incorporating its dispersed elements into a unified, comprehensive model is due to the Imam al-Shāfiᶜi.[152] It was his *Risalat* that established the four sources (usul) of Islamic law—the Qur'ān, tradition, consensus ('ijmaᶜ), and analogical deduction (qiyās)—in Muslim consciousness. I will examine the extent to which these sources

[152] Cf. Abdelmajid Sharfi, "al-Shafiᶜ Usuliyyan bayn al-Itibāᶜ wa al-Ibdāᶜ," *Labanat*, pp. 131-145. On Usul al-Fiqh see also Abdelmajid Sharfi, *Taḥdīth al-Fikr al-Islami* (Modernizing Islamic Thought).

are faithful to the Mission from a historical angle, but I will not discuss the sources as such, which would go beyond the limits of this study.

It should always be remembered that the use of the Qur'ān for the deduction of legal judgments implies a specific view of the text as a group of ready-made prescriptions, to be applied in every case. The Qur'ān, like all recorded texts (and in particular fundamental religious ones), is open to an almost infinite number of interpretations,[153] no matter how straightforward some of its verses seem to be. Nevertheless, the legal theologians ignored the intentions behind the conditional solutions offered by these verses and the specific contexts in which the āyāt (miracles) that they were studying occurred. Since a Muslim is a Muslim only if the Qur'ān is his guide, he needs a great deal of modesty and alertness to avoid projecting his own standards or inclinations–which are necessarily influenced by his personal situation and the general conditions–on the actual text. Yet, the prime characteristic of the legal theoreticians was certainty. They believed that the methodological, and especially linguistic, researches they had undertaken were sufficient to guarantee them the possession of absolute truth. Thus, they felt able to rule that the formulation of an issue indicated obligation in some cases and freedom of choice in others, when in fact they were only imposing their own values and concerns on the Qur'ān and carrying their interpretation too far. For example, they decided that the phrase "avoid it" (The Dinner Table 5/90) denoted the illicitness of intoxicants and the necessity of penalizing the drinker, while the phrase "write it down" (The Cow 2/282) gave Muslims the freedom to

[153] Cf. Al-Māwardi: "The words of every book and the message of every prophet are open to different interpretations, because that is the nature of speech. No speech is more so than the words of Almighty God, for they are the most eloquent, the briefest, the richest in symbols, and the most comprehensive of all" in ᶜAli Omlīl, *al-Muntadā*, Amman, no. 119, Sept. 1995, p. 3.

choose whether or not to make a note of a temporally fixed debt.

The obvious flaw in the theoreticians' treatment of the Qur'ān is that they separate the verses and take them out of both their specific and their general context. Their interpretation of the third verse of the Chapter of Women (4) is an obvious example. In the sentence beginning with "If you feel that you cannot act equitably towards orphans" and ending with "then marry such women as seem good to you, two and three and four" they willfully break the simplest rules of logic and grammar. At the same time, by allowing the man to marry four women, they disregard both the women's feelings about sharing their husband with others and the social disadvantages they suffer in such an event, and they close their eyes to the fate of the children, who may be brought up in an environment marked by quarrels between rival wives. Most importantly, they ignore those verses that develop a refined ethic of marriage in its Qur'ānic sense—that is, marriage based on mutal trust, love, mercy, and justice[154] and they fail to take into account the real reason for polygamy, which was the fear of not being able to treat the orphans equitably in certain circumstances.[155] The theoreticians' efforts, in this case and others like it, are nothing but an attempt to justify a common form of social behavior and to defend values which, I do not hesitate to say, are contrary to the Qur'ān. These

[154] I am not ignoring their directive that the man should distribute his nights equally and justly between his wives, but the equality and justice here are merely of a formal kind, since the man is not obliged to have the same amount of sexual intercourse with all his wives, so long as he does not neglect any one of them for more than four months.

[155] It is worth noting that we have no accounts that fully explain this particular issue, either in the books of exegesis or in the collections of ḥadīth. These accounts seem to have been left out deliberately because of the controversy they might arouse. It is likely that in the period before the opening of Mecca and the adoption of Islam by the Arab tribes, when the Muslims were few and in need of support, the Qur'ān confirmed a practice that was common in the Arab Peninsula before Islam.

values are merely founded on the consensus that has formed around them and involve no reliable reading and application of the text, as was falsely believed. In other words, the issue is not the reliance on the Qur'ān as one of the sources of Islamic law, but whether one interprets the Qur'ān in a manner consistent with its spirit and internal logic, or whether one insists on the literal meaning of a number of verses, which are manipulated and declared to be a faithful translation of the divine will and transcendent wisdom.

For the second source of legal theory, the Prophetic tradition transmitted through ḥadīth, I refer to the author of *al-Muqaddima*. In his chapter on the science of ḥadīth, Ibn Khaldūn states that "it is said that the number of traditions transmitted by Abu Ḥanīfah was only seventeen or so" (460) and that "Malik accepted as sound only the traditions found in the *Muwatta'*, of which there are at most three hundred or so." He further reports that Ibn Ḥanbāl "has 30,000 traditions in his *Musnad* (or even 40,000, according to two other editions of the *Muqadimmah*), selected "from among 750,000" (456).[156] These highly significant facts, which Ibn Khaldūn records with the matter-of-factness of the historian, are usually ignored by those who argue in favor of ḥadīth and tradition. I am not interested in how Khaldun explains the enormous discrepancies between what each of the Imams accepted as sound, because he merely repeats the ideas that had become ingrained in the Muslim mentality since the triumph of the traditionalists (Ahl al-Ḥadīth). What concerns me is the huge increase—from 17 to 30,000-40,000—in the number of supposedly "sound" traditions during the period between the first half of the second century and the first half of the third century after the hijra. Are these figures not enough to make one doubt the soundness of all these references to the Prophet, especially since they are all Aḥād ac-

[156] ᶜAbd El-Raḥman Ibn Khaldūn, *The Muqadimmah,* vol. 2, pp. 456-460.

counts[157] based on single authorities? The situation became so critical that the mere investigation of Ḥadīth, following al-Bukhāri and other collectors, ceased to be useful. The jurists could no longer do their work without resorting to the prophetic tradition, and when al-Shāfiᶜi sought to establish a firm code he was in fact responding to an unconscious collective desire by defending a specific view of the social system, which was in need of a religious justification not provided by the Qur'ān alone.

The objectors to this tendency were a minority, which soon dissolved in the broad current. We do not know the names, the numbers or the significance of the prominent figures among them, or whether any of their views were ever recorded. The only indication of their existence is found in the chapter entitled Jumaᶜ al ᶜIlm (the compilation of knowledge) in al-Shāfiᶜi's *al-Umm*, where one of them—who seems to be regarded as representative of the whole group—is quoted as asking: "How did you or anyone else find it permissible to say, about a matter decreed by God, first that the obligation is all-inclusive and then that it is one thing in particular, or first that it is an obligation and then that it is a question of meaning or whether or not the speaker desires something licit? I have often noticed how you attribute traditions to the authority of one person, then that of another, and another, until you finally ascribe it to the Prophet of God (may peace be upon him). I have also found that you and those who follow your ways credit nobody you meet with honesty and a reliable memory and deem nobody you cite to be immune from error and forgetfulness, but rather repeat

[157] The term Aḥād (one) indicates that the ancients doubted these accounts and did not consider them as sources of certified knowledge, while Tawatur (collective evidence) indicates that the accounts in question were widespread among people at a certain time, but this does not guarantee their soundness. Untrue rumors spread very fast, and it is no coincidence that modern positive laws do not depend on collective evidence to prove or disprove anything.

constantly: so-and-so is wrong about this tradition, and so-and-so about that. Moreover, if a man says of a tradition to which you have already referred and on which you have depended in your judgments about licitness and illicitness: 'The Prophet did not say this, and you, or those who have related this to you, are mistaken', you do not make him repent what he said and merely rebuke him. How is it permissible for an account by one, who is as you have described him, to cause disagreement about the judgments of the Qur'ān, when the outward meaning of the Qur'ān is one to all?" Al-Shāfi^ci continues the quotation as follows: "If you are determined to adopt these accounts despite all the flaws you have mentioned, how would you answer one who rejects them and says: 'I do not consent to any of these accounts if they are susceptible to delusion. I only consent to what bears testimony to God, as does His book, which is unquestionable and flawless'?" Unsurprisingly, in his lengthy response to this view, al-Shāfi^ci condemns any "failure to accept Ḥadīth and to insist that the Qur'ān contains clear indications (al-bayān)." That is his answer to the protestors' claim that he who carries out any act that falls under 'prayer' or 'zakāt', and who pays his dues and fulfills his duties regardless of the proper timing prescribed for these practices—even if he performs only two prostrations a day—is entitled to say: "If a matter is not mentioned in the book of God it is not an obligation."[158]

The objectors to tradition as an authority did not stand much of a chance because they were too radically opposed to the popular inclination towards the concrete, which resulted in the tendency to revert to the familiar mental frameworks of pre-Islamic times, and to magnify the role of Mohammed as an individual and a historical figure, with whom it was possible to identify, at the expense of his Mis-

[158] al-Imam Mohammad b. Idris al-Shāfi^ci, *al-Umm*, Beirut, 1973, vol. 7, pp. 273–276.

sion. Thus, many sayings and deeds ascribed to the Prophet were related neither to his personality as revealed in that most trusted of sources, the Qur'ānic text, nor to his era, which was marked by simplicity and spontaneity. In fact they were the product of the problems of a growing nation and the political and other disputes between its members. The historical conditions in which the legal theories were developed may not have allowed for more than partial differences between the major Islamic groups, in particular the Shi'ites, the Kharijites, and those known as 'Ahl al Sunna wa al Jamā^c^a' (the Sunnites), but each of these groups had its own approved chain of transmitters. The Shi'ites would only consider the accounts of their own Imams, and the Kharijites were very strict about the conditions of probity (^c^adālah) that must be fulfilled by their transmitters. Nevertheless, they condemned the Sunni traditionalists, saying: "We saw that these traditionalists criticize the transmitter for the slightest reason and that despite their awareness of grave slanders they accept the accounts of the companions and follow the accounts of the slanderers and the slandered alike. Religion is innocent of all this and these traditionalists are the devotees of the mighty and the slaves of the powerful; they supply accounts in favor of those in power and when the latter lose their power they desert them."[159] The Sunni traditionalists, in their turn, dismiss the accounts of their adversaries by calling them "Ahl al Ahwa' wal Bida^c^" (innovators and heretics). Nevertheless, if we exclude some particularly contentious issues, for instance those relating to the Imamate, it is noteworthy that the differences (ikhtilāf) in transmission did not lead to any major discrepancies in the corpus of these records. This phenomenon helped to unite the follow-

[159] Fakhreddin Al-Rāzī, *al-Maḥsūl,* 4/347. For their "epistemological" criticism of the transmission of ḥadīth, and their particular claim that the long period between the prophet's sayings and their transmission "necessarily discredits these accounts," see *al-Maḥsūl,* vol. 4, pp. 347-350.

ers of the different groups and schools despite their disagreements and disputes in some areas. Eventually they were all working on the same basis and by the same methods, even though these were a long way from the Mohammedan Mission's endeavor to combine divine love with human obedience and responsibility (with the latter denying neither divine love nor human freedom).

However, the consequences of the theoreticians' search for textual evidence were not always positive. On the one hand, the first generation never sought such evidence or regarded it as necessary. On the other hand, the development and changing conditions of civilization in the conquered regions gave rise to many cases without precedent from the time of the prophet or the period following it. This resulted in the recourse to consensus (ijmāᶜ)[160] as the third source of legislation where textual references were lacking. The legal theoreticians took great pains to prove the authority of this third source. They felt that in some cases, where relevant texts from the Qur'ān or established traditions were unavailable, other verses had been cited arbitrarily to create a tradition in response to the needs of the community rather than as a result of a genuine consensus. These traditions did not seem reliable enough, and therefore they resorted to concomitant traditions, which seemed to offer certitude by their own standards as well as those of the traditionalists.[161] This led to

[160] On consensus and disagreement see J. Van Ess, *Theologie und Gesellschaft im 2. und 3. Jahrhundert Hidschra,* Berlin and New York, 1990–1997, IV/654–660 (Konsens und Meinungsstreit).

[161] Thus, they were obliged to depend on both the concomitance of themes and the fact that these accounts were part of what the nation had unanimously agreed on. It is worth noting that al-Shāfiᶜi was unaware of that prophetic tradition which may be summed up in a phrase like "my nation does not agree upon error," which makes it likely that the tradition was not formulated until the third century after the hijra. On the other hand, it is also worth noting that Abu Ḥasan al-Ashᶜari "thought it possible to obtain certitude from one account ... and also thought it possible that many concomitant accounts may not present certain knowledge" (Ibn

the pitfall of a circular argument: consensus, as a source of legal theory, was founded on consensus. Al Ghazāli, as his *Mustasfā* shows, was aware of this pitfall and believed that it could be avoided by referring to the notion of custom (al-ᶜāda), but this did not solve the problem. Despite its shaky legitimacy, consensus was still considered the "source of sources." The Hanbalite jurist Ibn ᶜAqīl placed it above the text itself, because "consensus can be more conclusive than the text by one degree. Although the text is infallible in its wisdom, there may be another text which opposes and abrogates it ... whereas consensus is infallible and safe from opposition and abrogation, for there is none like it that can annul it."[162]

Regardless of the flaws of this argument, I must point out that consensus exists in both Christianity and Judaism, albeit under different names. All institutionalized religions need consensus, without which it would be very difficult to convince the congregation of believers of the validity of the rituals, doctrines, and unified ethics that the men of religion try to impose on them. In common with reliance on tradition as a source, reliance on consensus met an opposition that came to be regarded as a deviation once Islamic culture, with its essential constituents, had been firmly established. Although the books of Usūl repeatedly claim that the only thinker to reject consensus was al-Nazzām, this is most probably not the case. Moreover, these books neither specify the arguments used by al-Nazzām, or by others who took a similar stand, nor do they explain whether their arguments were related to the practical impossibility of consensus, its intrinsic weaknesses, or any other factor.[163] How-

Fork, *Mujarad Maqalāt al-Shaykh Abi Ḥasan al-Ashᶜari,* Beirut, 1987, p. 201.) The latter view is uncommon in the literature of usūl.

[162] Ibn ᶜAqīl, *al-Wādiḥ fi Usūl al-Fiqh,* Beirut, 1996, 1/20.

[163] Ibn al-Riwandi is probably the first to accuse al-Nazzām of denying consensus: "al-Nazzām claims that the whole nation of Mohammed may establish a false consensus on the basis of ra'y (reasoning) and qiyās, but

ever, in this study I am concerned with two different points:

The first point is the strange paradox between the theoreticians' premises and what they try to prove: they start with the consensus of the whole Islamic nation, which they believe to be indicated by the verse "And thus we have made you an exalted nation that you may be the bearers of witness to the people and that the Apostle may be the bearer of witness to you" (The Cow 2/143), but they end up proving the exclusive validity of the consensus of those scholars who apply personal reasoning. In doing so they specifically exclude the laity–above all, the women and the slaves[164]– whose views are not usually taken into consideration, particularly on issues that have been appropriated by those who claim to speak in God's name and to know His commands and prohibitions. According to their chief theoretician, this is "known only to scholars, and others are under no obligation to be familiar with it."[165] Such an obvious exclusion of the largest segments of society–and their subjection to such a guardianship–not only lacks any foundation in the Mohammedan Mission, but is also in complete opposition to the spirit of the Mission, which is addressed to all believers (men and women alike) without any kind of discrimination. That was what the Quraysh who embraced the Mission in its first phases refused to accept: "And when it is said to them: believe as the people believe, they say: shall we believe as the fools believe?" (The Cow 2/13).[166]

---

not on the basis of perception," *Fadiḥat al-Muᶜtazilah (The Scandal of the Muᶜtazilah)*, p. 120.

[164] On the status of women in the Islamic world in the Middle Ages see Gavin R. G. Hambly, ed., *Women in the Medieval Islamic World: Power, Patronage, and Piety*, MacMillan, 1998.

[165] al-Imam Mohammad b. Idris al-Shāfiᶜi, *al-Risāla fī Usūl al-Fiqh*, Majid Khadduri (trans.), UK, The Islamic Text Society, 1997, p. 28.

[166] Those who believed in Mohammed at the beginning of his Mission were not all "fools" (sufaha') (cf. Ḥayāt ᶜAmamo, *Asḥāb Mohammad wa Dawruhom fī Nash'at al Islām* [Mohammed's Companions and their Role in

The second point is that consensus can in itself carry the potential for change and prove a positive social force, if it is based on democratic ideas and if it corresponds to the inclinations of the majority with regard to matters of everyday life, such as clothes and food, as well as to broader economic and moral issues. The consensus of scholars in the second and third centuries after the hijra—which the theoreticians of the fifth century elaborated and laid down as the indisputable source of the law for successive generations—was intended to consolidate the solutions of a specific past, that is, the age of the Rashidun Caliphs and that of the companions and their successors. However, they did not consolidate that past as it really was, but rather as it had been reconstructed by scholars when the Qur'ān was recorded, making it appear perfect and obscuring all those features that revealed variety and dissent alongside unity and agreement. It was a past in which at some times the ruler imposed his personal opinions on his subjects, and at other times arguments were refuted by arguments, and truth was sought through honest debate. In other words, it had all the virtues and flaws of human history. Although the prophetic tradition of "what the Muslims see as good is good in the sight of God" is mentioned only in the Musnad (ḥadīth collection) of Ibn Ḥanbāl,[167] it is worthy of being taken as proof of the validity of consensus at times of hardship and trial, when consensus is needed, but not at times when differences of opinion are desirable, particularly when social circumstances change to such an extent that the new conditions no longer bear the slightest resemblance to the old ones.

---

the Rise of Islam, Tunis, 1996]), but the Quraysh nobles refused to mingle with them or to consider them their equals.

[167] Wensinck, *al-Muᶜjam li Alfāṭḥ al-Ḥadīth an-Nabawi*, second edition, Leiden, 1992, 1/368. al-ᶜIzz b. Abd el Salam says: "if this account proves sound then those meant by the Muslims here are the people of consensus (Ahl al-Ijmāᶜ)," *al-Fatawa*, Beirut, 1986, p. 42.

Given that similar causes have similar effects, the increase in the number of "occurrences" that are mentioned neither in the text nor in the tradition, analogy (qiyās) came to be considered as a fourth source of law. According to al-Shāfiʿi, there exists for "all matters touching the life of a Muslim, a binding decision or an indication as to the right answer."[168] If we rejected this postulate, which is as far as can be from the spirit of the Qur'ān; if we considered human actions as alternating between good and evil and being influenced by historical factors; if we recognized the significance of what is hidden behind external appearances; and if we realized that human freedom is the result of a constant search for ideal, necessarily progressive, ways of reconciling individual interests with the welfare of the group: if we did all this—which would seem obvious to the modern mind—the whole fundamentalist structure would collapse and there would be no use whatsoever for analogy (qiyās). Precedent, on which analogy is based, is not always a suitable root (source of law) for a loose branch (a judgement), particularly when the branch in its turn becomes a fixed root, that is, the judgment becomes a source of law on which a further analogy is based, and so on. How could this be a reliable procedure, when the decisions and judgments of jurists are as far removed from a consistent logic as possible? Despite their adherence to diverse tendencies and schools of thought, the objectors to the use of analogy realized long ago that it was impossible to apply analogy to the performance of rituals, which have no logical justification. The obligation on women to make up for any fasting day of Ramadan they miss as a result of menstruation, but not for any prayers they miss for the same reason, may serve as an example.[169] One of the

[168] al-Imam Mohammad b. Idris al-Shāfiʿi, *al-Risāla fī Usūl al-Fiqh*, p. 288. The 'binding decision' refers to everything that is compulsory, permissible, detested, or forbidden. Rewards and punishments in both the afterlife and this life depend on whether these 'decisions' are obeyed or flouted.

[169] I do not wish to examine these cases here. They are discussed in all

consequences of the recourse to analogy was the constant attention paid to the past, rather than to the present, let alone the future. Obviously, the present, with its prevalent values and its changing needs, is bound to have an effect on the perspective from which the past is viewed. Thus, analogy is never a neutral process and does not adhere to the principles of the Islamic Mission. The flaw lies in its very nature, even though jurists practicing it persist in claiming that it manifests the divine will, rather than admitting its justificatory role. The use of analogy, as of all other sources of law, for the purpose of proving the formal continuity between the age of the Prophet and the ages that followed has three grave consequences:

- Failure to achieve the ultimate goal of every legislative system, which is the establishment of a kind of justice that posits freedom and responsibility as essential conditions,[170]
- succumbing to the pitfall of allegations that do not stand up to historical criticism or honest objective reasoning,
- blocking the way for those who try to refer directly to the Qur'ān, without the mediation of jurists and exegetes.[171]

---

the classical works of legal theory, which devote either a chapter or part of a chapter to answering those who deny or object to *qiyās* as a source of law. Ibn Hazm al-Zahiri was known as one of the prominent objectors, and his opinion is evident in his *al-Iḥkām fī usūl al- Aḥkām.* As we have already seen, the disagreement between him and the followers of *qiyās* concerns the justifications of the Aḥkām (legal judgments) and not their existence.

[170] "To be just or unjust and to exercise justice, I must be free and responsible for my actions and my behavior, my thoughts, my decisions" (Jacques Derrida, "The Force of Law: The 'Mystical Foundation of Authority'," *Cardozo Law Review*, vol. 11, July–August 1990, p. 960.)

[171] Cf. Shaykh Mohammad al-Faḍil b. ᶜĀshour's statement that "the science of legal theory has in fact confined the schools and restricted the jurists, for it has limited the movement of Ijtihād," *Muḥāḍarāt*, Tunis, 1999, p. 346.

In general, Islamic legal theory has not developed much since the composition of the major monographs, Abu Husayn al-Basri's *al-Muᶜtamad,* Imam al-haramayn al-Juwaynī's al-*Burhān,* Ibn Hazm al-Zāhirī's al-*Aḥkām,* al-Ghazāli's *al-Mustasfā,* and al-Rāzī's *al-Maḥsūl.* Their successors relied on these monographs and, rather than making significant additions to them, explained, summarized, and supported the views of whichever school they belonged to, as did, for example, the Hanafites, who were unique in following Sukuni by tacit consensus, but at the same time joined some other schools in defending secondary sources of the law such as istiḥsān (legal preference), istisḥāb (presumption arising from accompanying circumstances), ᶜurf (custom), and *masālih mursalah* (general considerations of public interest). Ibn Isḥāq al-Shāṭṭibī's solitary attempt–in his *Muwāfaqat*–to pay heed to the intentions of religious law and not only to linguistic canonizations (*muwadaᶜāt*), would have been worth carrying further, but nobody elaborated on it or cleansed it of the traces of rigid fundamentalist thought. Mohammad Taher b. ᶜAshour's and ᶜAllāl al Fāsī's efforts reflect an awareness of the problem, but represent mere intentions rather than any real accomplishment capable of matching the models of ancient thought in this field.[172] In our own day, despite all the changes that have occurred in historical conditions and human knowledge, Islamic legal theory still ruminates over what the ancients said and rarely equals the depth and comprehensiveness of their monographs in its treatment of the issues concerned.[173]

[172] Mohammad al-Faḍil b. ᶜĀshour, *Maqasid al-Sharīᶜa al-Islamiyya,* republished in Tunis, 1366 after the hijra; ᶜAllāl al Fāsī, *Maqasid al-Sharīᶜa al-Islamiyya wa Makarimaha,* published many times in Morocco, see the 1963 edition. A comprehensive comparative and critical study of both can be found in: Nur el-din Buthuri, *Maqāsid al-Sharīᶜa: al-Tashrīᶜ al-Islami al-Muᶜasir bayn Tumūh al-Mujtahid wa Qusūr a-Ijtihād,* Beirut, Dar al-Taliᶜa, 2000.

[173] For a good evaluation of modern legal theology, see Mohammad Taᶜ Allah, *Kutub Usul al-Fiqh al-Ḥadīthā* (*Modern Books on Legal Theology)* (submitted for a DRA degree in the Humanities Department, Manuba, 1997).

QUR'ĀNIC EXEGESIS

It goes without saying that Qur'ānic exegesis cannot be separated from the other Islamic sciences. Like the others, it was gradually established as an independent discipline, and its practitioners were jurists, theologians, linguists, historians, and many more. All these fields of knowledge supported and complemented each other, and all these scholars were influenced by the same social values. They also had the same outlook on life in general and used similar methods in dealing with religion. They all believed that the Qur'ān was a book of laws that transcended time and space, and they all regarded the Mohammedan Mission as something that would liberate man from the fetters of imitating the fathers and forefathers, even if these were "the exemplary predecessors" (as-Salaf as-Sāliḥ). In their view, the Mission offered guidance on social behavior and urged man to take the responsibility for organizing his society, opening his eyes to the fact that the only absolute was God, and realizing that all the human historical and cultural phenomena were relative, inconstant, and subject to criticism, analysis, change, and amelioration.

By emphasizing the main features shared by Qur'ānic exegesis with other areas of Islamic thought, and by highlighting the presence, or absence, of certain reflections in it, I am in fact revealing the great differences between the Mission and its applications, and the sharp contrast between the concerns of the ancients and those of our own contemporaries. This is by no means intended to belittle the efforts of the past, to which we are much indebted, but rather to question the validity of past solutions, which were organically related to the conditions surrounding the ancients, for the present. These conditions differed substantially from our own conditions today, as do the conditions of all our contemporaries, regardless of their race, language, doctrines, beliefs, and civilizations, from those of their predecessors. I realize that by undertaking such a task I am challenging the natural human tendency to cling to the accustomed and the familiar, and to resist the novel and the unfamiliar. Since ancient times, religion has guarded against chaos and provided social institutions with legitimacy to the extent that they can no longer be easily imagined without the justifications of religion. It played this role not because it had created such an inclination, but because it was more effective and impressive than all the other legitimizing systems, which lack its solidity. As the uncertainty of life fills man with fear of death, it is no wonder that he should try to escape this tragic existential state of anxiety by searching for constancy and resorting to religion, which he believes can provide it. However, he fails to see the heavy price he pays for this security, which is both real and false at the same time. Can man pay a heavier price than giving up his essence, which makes him human? Man is a free and responsible creature, who descends to the level of animals once he loses his freedom and responsibility.

The traditional view of Qur'ānic exegesis is an idealistic one.[174] Based on the established legislative quality of the Mission, it is believed that the Prophet explained the obscure Qur'ānic judgments to his contemporaries, and that after his death his companions were more qualified than anyone else to interpret those Qur'ānic verses that were either too vague or too general to deal with individual cases. I do not believe that there was any necessity at all for the Prophet to interpret and explain the revelation, because his pronouncements were clear enough and mostly related to living experience. However, as time passed and conditions changed, Muslims came to believe that the Qur'ān alone did not suffice to provide the solutions required by institutionalized religion.

[174] Ibn Khaldūn expresses this view in the chapter on Qur'ānic exegesis in his *Muqadimmah*. The same view is also present in contemporary studies related to the history of this science, e.g. Mohammad Hussein al-Thahabi, *at-Tafsīr wa al-Mufassirun* (Exegesis and Exegetes), second edition, Cairo, 1976, 3 vols.

They attributed their own efforts at filling the "gaps" to Mohammed and his companions, justifying this imitation by quoting his own sayings—for example, "My companions are like the stars, whichever you follow, you will be rightly guided"—particularly when many of them began to see that things were moving in an undesirable direction and became increasingly nostalgic for the origins and the golden age in which everything was perfect.[175]

The need for Qur'ānic exegesis first appeared in two important areas: determining how rituals should be performed and, somewhat later, explaining those aspects of the tales of prophets and past nations that were left vague in the Qur'ān. With regard to rituals, the Qur'ān deliberately lacked the expected details, and therefore its verses were interpreted in the light of existing worship practices, which gradually acquired stereotypical features. The tales of the prophets were narrated as if they were actions and decrees of the Prophet himself and emphasized the necessity of following in his footsteps. In this respect the rule was to resort to those Ahl al-Kitab who embraced Islam—e.g. kaᶜb al-Aḥbār and Wahab b. Munabih—and who were acquainted with the books of the Jews and the Christians as well as their oral traditions, in which history was mixed with legend and fantasy. Consequently, Qur'ānic exegesis was infiltrated by so-called al-Israeliyyat, which will leave an indelible mark on exegesis, if modern historical knowledge is not correctly applied, and if the exegetes failed to distinguish between the fact that these tales were naturally influenced by the standards of knowledge that existed at the time of the Prophet and his followers, on the one hand, and the requirements of an exegesis fit for contemplation and speculation throughout the ages, on the other.

[175] Cf. Abdelmajid Sharfi, "Assalafiyya bayn al-Ams wa al-Yawm" (Orthodoxy between Yesterday and Today), in *Labanat*.

The search in the Qur'ān for validations of legal judgments concerning specific aspects of human behavior and social or economic interaction, and for textual evidence with regard to articles of faith—such as divine justice, the existence of evil in the world, man's freedom and responsibility for his actions, judgment day, and others—did not get under way until the beginning of the second century after the hijra, following the foundation of jurisprudence as an independent science and the establishment of speculative theology with its intellectual (ᶜaqli) and traditional (naqli) areas of studies. Every group and theological school manipulated the text, projecting its own established theories and doctrines on it, and deciding that certain verses were valid, while others were void or suspect. The exegetes disregarded the essential difference between revelation, which is by nature based on symbol and metaphor, and conceptualization, which generally characterizes human knowledge. Eventually, the different interpretations became indispensable mediators of the Qur'ānic text, solidifying into a body of secondary literature that impeded any direct understanding of the Qur'ān and free individual reasoning.

The linguistic—lexical, grammatical, and stylistic—analysis of the texts was not used as a basis or starting point for these interpretations, but rather as an accessory to justify the different, or even contradictory, choices they represented. For instance, al-Zamakhshari's linguistic concerns did not prevent him employing the Qur'ān in defense of his Muᶜtazili views, while the Sunnites, al-Tabari and al-Rāzī, or the Shi'ites, at-Tusi and at-Tabarsi, applied linguistic criteria to the text in order to defend some diametrically opposed standpoints. If a text is to be understood it must follow the specific rules of the language in which it is written. Nevertheless, it will inevitably carry a variety of meanings reflecting the different expectations and circumstances of each reader. The Qur'ān, according to a famous saying by ᶜAli b. Abu Tālib, "does not speak, but is made to speak by men."

Thus, the real purpose of exegesis was to interpret the text within the boundaries prescribed by the particular doctrinal sect and juristic school to which each exegete belonged. Although exegesis was thought of as an open science, it ruled out any attempt at personal reasoning (ijtihadāt) that went beyond the historically approved limits of disagreement. This may be the reason why Muslims through the ages have been intent on composing exegeses, while the reader feels that all these exegeses contain the same material, repeated over and over again, with only slight adjustments and additions. Ever since exegesis became a separate art or "craft," all exegetes have believed that they were obliged to adhere to the order of ayas and suras as they appear in the Muṣḥaf (copy of the Qur'ān), and they did not allow themselves (or rather their circumstances did not allow them) to come up with fresh suggestions or follow different paths, which–depending on each exegete's capabilities–might have led to a new understanding of the Qur'ān's purposes and themes.

Most of the men who embarked on exegesis were either elderly–which explains why many of the exegeses were left incomplete–or experienced in Qu'rānic studies, i.e. those fields of study that were restricted to deduction (istinbāt) by the established methods, in addition to the history of the Muṣḥaf, the sciences of language and recitation, the Israeliyyat, the conflicting traditions, the explanations of the jurists, and interpretations going back to popular oral culture.[176] In the process, the ultimate purpose of the Mission was lost, and the text became a mere excuse for defending values that were usually neither related to nor required by it.

[176] For example, see al-Baydawi's interpretation of the seventh verse of the chapter of Ad-ḍuḥa (93): "Did he not find you lost and show you the way." Observe how the exegete here, in accordance with popular Islamic consciousness, declines to admit that the prophet was 'not on the right way' in a spiritual sense before the revelation and prefers the literal meaning of "lost" by relating this verse to the time when Mohammed lost his way home after going in search of a stray sheep.

Al-Tabari may have hesitated between boldly repeating the words of God as if he were speaking in His name (for example when he begins his interpretation of a verse with a phrase such as "God Almighty says") and adopting a less direct approach (for example, when he suggests that a certain understanding of a verse is "most likely to be true, in my opinion"). Nevertheless, it was the former approach that came to dominate exegesis in general, which was marked more and more by excessive confidence and the exclusion of all that the exegete regarded as incompatible with his own choices and those of his school.

The great, open-minded Fakhreddin al-Rāzī did not ignore the difficulties he encountered, but acknowledged them frankly and tried to overcome them, either by considering his subject from all angles and employing his encyclopedic knowledge of the various fields of study known in his age, or by entrusting the issue to God and admitting his failure when he could not offer a logical and convincing solution. Nevertheless, even he was not entirely able to escape the influence of the established traditional culture that hampered all attempts at a direct reading of the text independently of earlier exegeses.[177] In other words, exegesis constituted a complete system of firmly linked elements, not one of which could be removed without upsetting the whole structure. This explains the resistance of the traditionalists, whenever a new standpoint, which is incompatible with the system, emerges. They seem to forget that the system itself

[177] It is worth noting here that the difficulties that arise in dealing with the text differ with the times. An instructive example is provided by verses 36 and 37 in the chapter of at Tawba (9), which concern the number of months in a year and the postponement of the sacred month (an-nasī'), described as "an addition to unbelief." These two verses created no difficulties for the ancient exegete, whereas today's Muslim has the right to wonder about their descent and purpose, especially since the judgment they carry reflects on the period in which fasting and Ḥajj are performed. The fact is that the Arabs before Islam practiced an-nasi' in order to ensure that the Hajj would always take place in spring.

developed historically in response to circumstances and values that were very different from those of today's Muslims. This fact, which they have constantly disregarded, gives license for a new interpretation of the Qur'ān, which would take account of the progress of human knowledge and operate on a basis other than the established system that now burdens Islamic thought.

ḤADĪTH

I have already touched on many issues related to the Prophetic tradition (ḥadīth), in particular as a source of Islamic law. At this point I will discuss it only as one of the Islamic sciences and of the constituents of the Islamic system. One rarely finds so great a difference between the common linguistic meaning of a word and its meaning when used in a specific technical sense, as in the case of ḥadīth and Sunna. These two terms, in the course of time, have undergone such a development that they are now interchangeable. They both refer to the words, actions, and decrees of the Prophet as recorded in the collections of ḥadīth by the Ahl al Sunna in the third century after the hijra.[178]

A somewhat strange aspect of the ḥadīth is that they actually contain indications of the Prophet's prohibition on recording them and his command that none of his words should be recorded in the Qu'rān. In other words, the ḥadīth themselves preserve the message that destroys their legitimacy as a science. The Prophet wanted the Qu'rān to be the

[178] Cf. Mohammad Ḥamza, al-*Ḥadīth an-Nabawi wa Manzilatuhu fi al-Fikr al-Islami al-Ḥadīth* (Prophetic Tradition and its place in Modern Islamic Thought), (submitted for a DEA degree in the Department of Humanities, Manuba, 1992); Ḥamadi Thuwaib, a*s-Sunna Aslan min Usul al-Fiqh Ila Nihayat al-Qarn al-Khamis al-Hijri* (Sunna as a Source of Juristic Theory until the Fifth Century after the Hijra) (submitted for a DRA degree in the Department of Humanities, Manuba, 1993).

Muslims' sole guiding light both in life and after death, and he did not want his words to acquire a peremptory normative quality. However, the Muslims desired the very opposite, although we must recognize that what kept them from obeying was as much the novelty of the Prophet's demands as their own unpreparedness to take the responsibility for organizing their lives. It is quite evident that the first generation of Muslims generally observed the prohibition on recording the sayings they heard. Those of the Prophet's companions who did record them kept them as blessed tokens for themselves, without any intention of disseminating what they had written down. Nor is it a mere coincidence that the infringement of the Prophet's wish was attributed to ᶜUmar b. ᶜAbd al-ᶜAzīz, the fourth Rashidun Caliph, who was regarded as the very embodiment of piety and uprightness, and who was therefore able to secure the necessary backing for his actions. From the Sunni perspective, it was al-Zahri who undertook the task of recording the ḥadīth, and thus became first to tread the path that others, whether reliable transmitters or mere composers of traditions, were later to follow.

The first written collections of ḥadīth date back to the same period as the first written records in other areas of knowledge, and in particular pre-Islamic poetry, on which the linguists primarily depended in formulating and systematizing the language. Naturally, this poetry contained many archaic words and unusual structures, which needed to be explained, just as a number of Qur'ānic terms and phrases were in need of interpretation. However, it is noteworthy that the major linguists in the second century after the hijra, despite their belief in the Prophet's eloquence, did not regard the ḥadīth as an authority and relied on them neither for the formulation of rules nor for explanation or interpretation. They doubted that the traditions ascribed to the prophet had been transmitted word for word, especially since the Prophet's own era was separated from the era of recording by more than a century, and the majority of transmitters were not Arabs. How could they have trusted these traditions when they saw their numbers increase daily?

The spread of false composition was sufficient reason for the disregard of ḥadīth in linguistic matters and for investigations into ḥadīth collections, which gradually acquired a holy status similar to that of the Qur'ān, with the result that the mere label "related by the two sheikhs" (meaning Bukhārī and Muslim), was regarded as the guarantee of the soundness of a tradition. Imam Malik lived in Ḥijāz, where the deliberate composition of ḥadīth was relatively rare, and therefore he only recorded some three hundred traditions when he sought references for the legal judgments in his *Muwatta'*. That is why his book was thought to be "the soundest after the book of God." Bukhārī, Muslim, and the other compilers of ḥadīth collections in the third century after the hijra were in a very different position. From all the traditions that reached them they only selected a small number that fulfilled the conditions of soundness. The Shi'ite compilations from the fourth century after the hijra were supposed to rest on the exclusive authority of the Imams, but in fact they only differ from the Sunni compilations with respect to a limited number of subjects.

The criteria of soundness in the era of recording were not yet fixed and codified to be applied mechanically. The compilers had to develop these criteria through their own reasoning and reflection. All available evidence suggests that they were models of honesty, uprightness, and objectivity, who only hoped for rewards in the afterlife. They refrained from criticizing the content or the formulation of the traditions ascribed to the Prophet and they did not reveal their personal opinion of what they related. That is why they inevitably focused on the chain of transmission rather than on the message itself in their attempts at certifying the soundness of the large number of traditions they sought to collect.

As the condition for the acceptance of a tradition, the ḥadīth scholars stipulated that every link in the chain of transmission should be represented by a known individual, rather than by a vague reference or an abstract adjective. As a further condition, they demanded that the transmitter should be of an age that allowed him to distinguish between his different informants, and have a reputation for his good memory and accuracy. Yet another condition was that he should be known for his probity (*ᶜadālah*), and that his behavior should not be stained with anything that might violate the laws of manliness or chivalry,[179] or associate him with innovators and heretics. Thus, the criteria for the soundness of ḥadīth collections were gradually established and became one of the ḥadīth scholars' major concerns, called the science of Jarḥwa Taᶜdīl (personality criticism).

Initially, the ḥadīth scholars did not take much notice of the manner in which the tradition was delivered to them, but in the course of their investigations they felt obliged to pay more and more attention to this aspect. As a result, they distinguished between mursal (in which the first transmitter after Mohammed is passed over), munqatiᶜ (in which one link is omitted), marfuᶜ (in which the tradition is traced back to Mohammed himself), and other forms of ḥadīth transmission. Further distinctions were made between ḥadīth related in private and those related in a group, and between ḥadīth read from a written document and those recalled from memory. Yet more distinctions included that between Ijāzah (the sheik's permission for his student to teach certain traditions) and Munawala (the sheik's written approval), and those between different introductory phrases—such as "I was told," "we were told," "it was related to me," "it was related to us," "based on so and so," "I heard from so and so," "I read in so and so"—that gradually acquired the status of technical terms only recognized by experts. From each of these forms

[179] It is worth noting that this was a pre-Islamic feature before it was "Islamicized." Therefore it reflects social values that were closely related to the life of Arabs in the Arab Peninsula. For example, eating in the street in public was thought to be a personality flaw and would have disqualified the person concerned as a transmitter.

of narration, something can be deduced about the authenticity of the ḥadīth, which may be described as sound, good, weak, irregular etc., although eventually these classifications were merely used to support one particular doctrine or another.

The different kinds of research included in the "Sciences of ḥadīth"[180] prove that the soundness and authenticity of the Prophetic tradition was a problematic issue even for the first exponents. As Ibn Qutayba's book *Ta'wil Mukhtalif al-ḥadīth*[181]—written after the era of codification—shows, the concentration on formal aspects was in fact a way of hiding the contradictions, irrationalities, and deviations from Qur'ānic teaching found in the ḥadīth, not to mention their awkward phrasing and their redundancies. To resolve these problems and to reconcile the different accounts, a number of scholars took upon themselves the task of "interpreting" the ḥadīth collections. They made great efforts to defend and present them in a manner compatible with the established doctrines, judgments, and postulates, deploying the utmost linguistic and historical expertise in the process.

If one examines the ḥadīth closely, one cannot help making the following disturbing observations:

- Ḥadīth is one of the sciences of tradition (Naql), in which there is no room for reasoning. The Muslim can only accept those traditions on which the nation agrees by consensus. This takes no account of the fact that what is generally accepted is merely accepted by a certain group, which has triumphed over the others for reasons unrelated to the soundness of its choices, and that the process of collecting, classifying, and recording, is in itself a matter of choice. By definition, choice means adopting some things and exclud-

[180] The classical work of reference on this is Ibn Salāḥ's al-Muqaddimah, which has appeared in many editions in Beirut and Cairo (for instance, Cairo, 1991).

[181] For instance, the Cairo, 1982, edition.

ing others, and this could not happen without an implicit critique of the content of ḥadīth and of the personality of the transmitter, even if the ḥadīth scholar claimed to be solely criticizing the chain of transmission.[182] What was finally adopted reflected the image of the Prophet in the period after the revelation and at the same time represented a projection of the values exclusive to the circles of ḥadīth scholars.

- The material of ḥadīth monographs was not restricted to words and actions ascribed to the Prophet but also contained words and actions of his companions, which were credited with a normative quality similar to the Prophet's. Moreover, the notion of "companionship" was broadened to include all those who had ever seen the Prophet, even if on a single occasion. All were invested with the same qualities of perfection and infallibility as those who had believed in him, supported him, and accompanied him for long periods. This link in the chain of transmission, unlike the rest, was not subject to personality criticism.

- The Ḥadīth were treated in the same manner as the Qur'ān, and both were considered to have the same degree of authenticity. Thus, they were followed literally, learnt by heart, and read without any reflection. They were studied, particularly in jurisprudence, according to the same criteria as the verses of the Qur'ān—whether abrogated or abrogating, general or specific, obscure or detailed, etc.—without considering the understandable reservations concerning the circumstances of their recording.

This does not mean that the Prophetic Tradition, as it has reached us, is futile. It is indeed a rich repository of noble, eternal insights. However, it contains both evergreen and desiccated branches, both valuable and worthless elements, both mere echoes of traditional social concerns and princi-

[182] *Pace* Subḥī al-Ṣāliḥ's claim, in *ᶜUlūm al-Ḥadīth*, Beirut, 1956, that the criticism of Ḥadīth deals with both the content and the chain of transmission, even though his book is written from a traditional perspective.

ples valid for all times and places. That is why it needs to be questioned and sifted. There is no escape from subjecting it to a criticism illuminated by the directives of the Mission and free from any canonization or literal reading of the text. It is the only way to ensure that it will continue to live.

SPECULATIVE THEOLOGY (ᶜILM AL-KALĀM)

The crisis of Islamic sciences as viewed from a contemporary perspective was, perhaps, the result of the overlap between jurisprudence, exegesis, and ḥadīth, on the one hand, and speculative theology, on the other.[183] Theology has been established in Muslim consciousness—in accordance with Ibn Khaldūn's definition in the sixth chapter of his *Muqaddimmah*—as "the science which involves arguing with logical proofs in defense of the articles of faith and refuting the innovators who deviate from the dogmas of the early Muslims and Muslim orthodoxy" (vol. 3, 34). This definition can stand for the entire output of the theologians, especially those elements that were corroborated by the Muᶜtazilah and that infiltrated many of the postulates of Sunni theology, such as the ash-Shᶜarite and the Matridian. It stresses the defensive quality of theology, assuming that "articles of faith" are an established given, which is only in need of "logical proofs". The historical truth is very different. Modern scholars are unanimous that there was a close relationship between the political circumstances after the great strife over the Caliphate (al-fitnah al Kubra) and the first attempts at theorizing that unprecedented condition, which was marked by power struggles and disputes among the companions. However, there is no agreement as to the correct judg-

[183] The best modern studies of ᶜIlm al-Kalām are, in Arabic, Ḥasan Mahmud al-Shafīᶜi, *ᶜIlm al-Kalām*, second edition, Cairo, 1991, and in German, J. van Ess, Theologie und Gesellschaft (six volumes, devoted entirely to Islamic religious thought in the second and third centuries after the hijra).

ment on either the parties that were fighting or those that remained neutral.

Although these events were a direct cause of the emergence of the first theological studies, many of the Qur'ānic verses were bound to provoke speculation and reflection, particularly after the development of the faith from the spontaneous stage to a rationalized one. The verses concerned were those dealing with fate, predestination, the existence of evil in the world, the Day of Judgment, and other questions that inevitably arise in the context of any religious thought and by nature need time to take root and to be internalized. However, the process of internalization can only take place within the boundaries of a people's culture, whether inherited or acquired though interaction with other cultures. In the Islamic context, it was through the combination and integration of these various elements, on the one hand, and the given text, on the other, that speculative theology emerged. We should always keep this in mind, lest we fall prey to the illusion that theology is autonomous and transcends time and space. The risk of such a misconception is due to the absolute quality ascribed to theology once it had acquired its own methods and postulates, and become subject to its own internal logic, to the extent that its topics mutually generated each other and the controversy surrounding them left its traces in the solutions that were destined to be disseminated and promulgated in due course. This fact is the opposite of the common belief that the first theologians were in possession of the sound doctrine, before "suspicions" and innovations emerged, spreading error and heresy. In reality, the prevalent orthodox doctrine was the outcome of the clash between different exegeses and only came into existence by virtue of those controversies: that is why it retains part of these exegeses and rejects other parts in accordance with the position it is trying to support. Thus, Ibn Khaldūn's statement that "speculative theology is not something that is necessary to the contemporary scholar [because] heretics and innovators have been destroyed" (54) only reveals his delusion as a result of the fossilization of thought in his time, which he seemed to regard as a positive feature, whereas in fact it was only a sign of the stagnation that precedes death.

The defensive features that marked theology in later phases obscured its true and essential task of attemping to interpret and clarify the given revelation, not by blindly following orthodox views, but rather by allowing each generation to employ the achievements of human knowledge in its own time, whether or not these agree with the established ideas. That is why philosophy, history, sociology, psychology, phonetics, and other sciences must neither compete with theology nor be subservient to it. Each of these sciences has its special field of study, with its special methods, premises, and conclusions. The theologian must not overlook these, but must take advantage of them, or else there would be a large gap between his knowledge and that of his time, and people would not be able to understand him or relate to what he says, even if they blindly memorized it.[184] In particular, he should ask what is outdated and no longer compatible with the knowledge and sciences of his day. Long ago Al-Jāḥiz famously stated: "The theologian cannot have a full grasp of theology nor be an expert at his craft and eligible for leadership, unless he is as knowledgeable in religion as he is in philosophy. The true scholar, we maintain, is he who combines both."[185]

Following the main direction of this work, I do not intend to study the history of this—or any other—Islamic science, but rather to explore its relationship with the Mohammedan Mission, as I portrayed it earlier. In this respect, three major features are worthy of note:

[184] Cf. the notes in L Bras, "Réflexions sur les différences entre sociologie scientifique et sociologie pastorale," *Archives de sociologie des religions*, 8 (1959), pp. 5-14. See also Muna Ahmad Abu Zayd's comments about the role of ʿIlm al-Kalām, in *al-Fikr al-Islami ʿind Ibn Khaldūn* (Ibn Khaldūn's Islamic Thought), Beirut, 1977, pp. 32-36.

[185] Al Jāḥiẓ, *Al Ḥayawān*, 2/134-135.

- The first feature is that theology, as revealed in the works of its practitioners in various sects, is not a purely Islamic science, but both Islamic and Greek. Although the theologians' aim—in Judge ᶜAbd el-Jabbar's[186] phrase—was "to present what would advocate monotheism and justice," the tools they used were the postulates and logic of Greek philosophy. Tools are never innocent or neutral, but doubtless influence and point their object in a direction that would be different if the tools themselves were different. That is what the scholars of ḥadīth, and all those who rejected philosophy and denied the agreement between its concepts and those of orthodox faith, were aware of. Needless to say, the logic of the Greeks, and other ancient peoples, is very different from modern logic; in particular it is the product of a mathematical knowledge that has entirely lost its validity in the light of the great progress of that discipline, above all in the last two centuries. The same applies to many of those postulates and concepts of philosophy known as the "subtleties" explicitly or implicitly employed in the "sublimities," that is the study of divinity, prophethood, the afterlife, the oneness of God, and various other subjects that seem to be religious, or indeed purely Islamic, but are in fact reflections of astronomy, geography and the other natural sciences. These sciences were products of their times and have merely historical value as devices used by the Muslim scholars of the first centuries to translate the content of the faith into a commonly understood language, but which later became mere food for rumination in the ages of intellectual decadence.

- The second feature is that theology was marked from its beginnings by a tendency towards sharp debates over issues that should have been dealt with cautiously and humbly. These differences in opinion regularly led to accusations of atheism and heresy, as theologians generally tried to refute

[186] ᶜAbd el-Jabbar b. Ahmad, *Faḍl al-Iᶜtizal,* Tunis, 1973, p. 185.

the arguments of their adversaries by all possible means, without examining the soundness or falseness of the stances they were defending, and regardless of the contradictions or distortions of the truth that these stances may have contained. Abu Ḥanīfah describes the situation in his time as follows: "We used to argue as if there were birds perched on our heads [i.e. very cautiously] lest our adversary should slip. You argue desiring your adversary to slip. He who desires his opponent to slip in fact intends to lead him into heresy, and he who aims at leading his opponent into heresy becomes a heretic himself."[187] However, those ḥadīth scholars who rejected theology and thought of the Muᶜtazilah, and of theologians in general, as heretics were no better. Ibn Ḥanbāl, for example, bluntly declares: "These are the doctrines of the people of knowledge ... Whoever deviates from them or contests them or finds fault in them is a heretic, an apostate, and a deviator from Sunna and truth."[188] By and large, excessive confidence, or rather dogmatism,[189] prevailed and left no room for free personal reasoning. All believed that the truth already existed and a Muslim had to do nothing but uncover it. All believed that the truth existed behind man or above him, but not before his eyes.

- The third feature is the interrelation between theology and politics. Some of the first theologians opposed the Umayyid rule and paid for their opposition with their lives, as did for example Ghaylan al-Dimashqi, Jaᶜd b. Dirham, and al-Jahm b. Safuan.[190] Likewise, some of the Muᶜtazilites were

[187] Ibn Bazāz al-Kurdi, *Manāqib al-Imam al-Aᶜtham Abu Ḥanīfa*, Hyderabād, 1331 after the hijra, 1/122.

[188] Ibn Abi Yaᶜla, *Tabakāt al-Ḥanābila*, Cairo, 1998, 1/24.

[189] On this central topic in sociology, see Milton Rokeach's article "The Nature of Dogmatism and its Significance" in *Psychology Review*, (1954), 61, no. 8, pp. 194-204.

[190] The first was killed in the Caliphate of Hishām b. ᶜAbd el-Malek with the approval of al 'Uzaᶜi, the second is the one Khaled b. ᶜAbdullah al-Qasri "sacrifice" in the year 124 or 125 of the hijra, and the third was killed in the year 128 of the hijra. See their biographies in the Encyclope-

in favor of the Abbasid rule before it turned on them. However, the overall course adopted in Sunni theology from the mid-fourth century after the hijra by the followers of al-Ashᶜari and al-Matrīdī was characterized by the defense of positions that seemed faith-related but in fact were political. By advocating blind obedience, whether deliberately or inadvertently, these theologians served the interests of the rulers. This is a particularly noticeable effect of al-Baqlāni's, ᶜAbd el-Qaher al-Baghdadi's, and al-Ghazāli's efforts to establish man's lack of volition and to deny causality, on the grounds that both of these restrict God's power and contradict the miracles of the prophets. The Jabriyya belief in predestination is in essence an echo of what Muᶜawiyya said when he became a ruler: "If God did not see me fit for this, He would not have left it to me; if God hated this for me, He would have given it to another."[191] With the help of these, and many other, justifications of oppression and tyranny, whole generations of Muslims were taught not to analyze human actions and trace them back to their obvious social causes, but rather to hark back to the first cause in its simplest and most dangerous form, believing that ignorance is a sign, or indeed a requirement, of piety, and thus allowing all forms of dependency, superstition, subjugation, and radicalism to spread and put down roots.

SUFISM

If rational perceptions are the basis of speculative theology (al-Kalām), emotion is that of Sufism in Islam, and indeed of all religious systems, whether in the east or in the west. In the third century after the hijra Muslim scholars were exer-

---

dia of Islam (in English and French); and in Al-Zarkali, *Al-Aᶜlām*, Beirut, Dar al ᶜIlm lil Malayin (many editions) 8 vols., and in J. Van Ess, *Theologie und Gesellschaft*, op. cit.

[191] ᶜAbd el-Jabbar b. Ahmad, *Faḍl al-Iᶜtizal*, op. cit., p. 143.

cised by the dichotomy between philosophy and religious law and a parallel dichotomy between the search for truth and religious law. In both cases Islamic thought saw many attempts at reconciliation, which eventually resulted in the dismissal of philosophy as an independent field of study, with logic and metaphysics alone being retained. This process also affected Sufism and curbed its extravagances by only allowing it to concern itself with the esoteric and the arcane on condition that it acknowledged, at least formally, the importance of the exoteric and the necessity of respecting it.

Almost all Sufis agree that their experience defies language, that is why they often resort to poetry, aphorisms, and proverbs. Their writings are full of symbols, signs, and allusions, and they attach to ordinary speech hidden connotations and special meanings that differ from the literal ones. As a result of its peculiar rationale and its profuse imaginative features, Sufism is very hard to evaluate. The utmost a scholar can hope for is to appreciate Sufism as a socio-political phenomenon that from time to time played a major role in shaping the political, economic, and social, as well as the intellectual, life of the community. This approach is likely to neglect the spiritual dimension essential to Sufism, which may vary in sincerity and intensity, but which tries to penetrate to the depth of the Mohammedan Mission—and indeed of all prophetic missions—and to transcend time and space, take refuge in "taste" rather than reason, and break free from the chains and fetters of those who appoint themselves "guards of the temple."

If one looks for the origins of Sufism,[192] one can easily find them in the tendency towards asceticism which accompanied the inclination of a group of believers in all religions to

[192] I will not enlarge on the many specific studies of Sufism, because my purpose is not to trace the history of this "science" but rather to investigate the extent of its responsiveness to the Mohammedan Mission. Probably the best is Annemarie Schimmel, *Sufismus*, Munich, 2000.

disengage themselves from worldly concerns and the burdens of livelihood, and to express their readiness for physical death and annihilation. This propensity was nourished by meditating upon those Qur'ānic verses that urge the Muslim to beware of this transient world and to look ahead to the approaching afterlife, in addition to those verses that warn against gathering silver and gold and failing to spend it in God's cause, and those that promise heaven to the good and the charitable, and threaten heretics with hell and eternal suffering. The tendency towards asceticism was actually present in the generation of the companions and many of them, whose traits are mentioned in their biographies, were famous for it. It also existed in subsequent generations, although in their case it was rather marginal and only influenced a small number of individuals who were known for their extreme piety and their habit of retiring to isolated shrines and cells in order to pray and worship.

Even without Sufism this form of asceticism would probably have persisted, nourishing Islamic sentiment and accompanying the contemplation of the teaching of the Qur'ān and the imitation of the ways of the Prophet. Likewise, it would have continued to displease those who believed it possible to bridle men's thought and imagination, forcing diverse outlooks and inclinations into the same ready-made mold or weaving different kinds of thread into the same cloth. However, it would never have developed into Sufism—i.e. a particular kind of uniform behavior based on a set of rules shared by a whole community—but for two concurrent factors, which combined to give rise to a movement that went beyond mere asceticism:

- The first factor was the spread of extravagance and indulgence in luxurious clothing, food, and houses, in addition to profligacy and debauchery,[193] as a result of prosperity un-

[193] Al-Washā', *al-Muwasha 'aw al-Thurf wa al-Thurafa',* Beirut, 1999, re-

der the Abbasid rule. These unfamiliar modes of behavior, which accompanied the inroads of civilization into a simple unsophisticated culture, provoked those who were unable to adjust to it, and caused them to turn their back on all the values it produced. There is a sense in which Sufism was a mere reaction to everyday reality and not the pursuit of a preconceived idea. Thus, like all reactions, it was bound to go to the other extreme, rejecting all the amenities of worldly life, both the licit and the illicit–except for marriage. Marriage was a notable exception, because celibacy was not part of the Prophet's conduct, and because it was a sign of Christian monasticism, with which the Sufis did not wish to be associated. That is why they did not abstain from marriage any more than other segments of society.

- The second factor was the jurists' appropriation of the prerogative of translating the requirements of faith into external practices designed to guarantee the unity of the group. While that form of worship normally satisfied those committed to the material aspects of life, it failed to offer the spiritual nourishment required by others, who felt a need for more than exoteric practices and rituals, and who longed for a clear conscience, tranquility, and harmony between the real and the desired. The Sufis had restless souls and surging emotions, which made them strive to comprehend the secrets of existence. Many therefore preferred isolation and detachment from worldly concerns, practising introspection and other forms of spiritual exercises they expected to release them from the prison of the body and to carry them to highest levels of certitude and closeness to God.

The Sufis' existential quest was untrammeled by any constraints and directives, and thus it was natural for them to develop theories and attitudes that deviated, in varying de-

---

flects the extent of the sophistication and luxuries of that time. The profligacy is reflected in the poetry of Wābila b. al-Ḥabāb, Abu Nuwās, and others.

grees, from the forms and contents of the faith set by the scholars and assented to by the public. By breaking free from rituals and compulsions, and claiming divinity through unity or incarnation, they provoked the anger of the jurists, who sought the aid of the political authority in confronting them. The trial of al-Ḥallāj and his crucifixion in 309 after the hijra signaled the end of one phase and the beginning of another in the history of Sufism. The first phase was characterized by its emergence from asceticism as an independent intellectual movement on the margin of the juristic schools and the political and doctrinal groups. The second phase was marked by an increase in the number of its followers, particularly once the prominent Sufi figures had managed to obtain the acquiescence of jurists, and the holy men in general, by acknowledging the latter's right to attend to the flesh of the religion, albeit not to the core. However, this tactical retreat did not save Sufism from being infiltrated by Gnostic ideas and influenced by illuministic (Ishrāqiyya) philosophy, which supplied Ahl as-Sunna, and other defenders of the purity of the doctrine and the emulation of orthodoxy, with reasons for maintaining their reservations and using force against some of the Sufi leaders, for example Shahab al-Din al-Sahrawardi, who was killed in 586 after the hijra.

Despite the many objections, Sufism acquired an important position that led Muslims of all social classes to embrace it, and seek to advance in its "stations," thanks to the efforts of al-Ghazāli, who established it among the Sunni, and other prominent figures, such as the 'Great Sheikh' Muhieddin b. ᶜArabi. However, it would not have spread as it did throughout the Islamic world without its hierarchical organization, which subjected the novices (*murīdūn*) to the will of their sheikh, and without its gatherings for the performance of rituals and collective exercises. This feature strengthened the bonds between the Sufis and ensured the uniformity of their behavior.

Like all organizations that lack democratic rules to direct them, Sufism eventually calcified, and from the sixth century after the hijra, gradually assumed the advantages and disadvantages of any organization. One of its major advantages was the effective framework it provided for the social classes at a time when political divisions prevailed and learning and education were restricted to towns and cities, excluding rural areas. In addition, many of the Sufi leaders played a significant role in defending the weak and unfortunate, and in resisting foreign invasions, which continued until recent times, as for instance in the case of Prince ᶜAbd el Qader and French colonialism in Algeria, and that of the Sanusis and Italian colonialism in Libya. However, the disadvantages inherent in organization destined Sufism to be one of the fiercest enemies of the reformation movement in the nineteenth century. The interaction of Sufism with popular forms of belief and pagan doctrines—together with the growing ignorance, superstition, and divisions among its sheiks—is likely to have been responsible for the spread of a sense of subservience and a belief in miracles (Karamāt) attributed to saints and holy men.

Thus, Sufism, in the course of history, evolved as a two-sided phenomenon. On the one hand, it offered many of its followers rich and satisfying spiritual experiences, allowing them to rise to high levels of intellectual ecstasy, evident in their admired works, which remain a source of inspiration for Muslims and non-Muslims. On the other hand, it represents a state of reclusion and an escape from confronting, and trying to improve, reality. Thus, for all its merits in dealing with the Mission, it has become one of the causes of the present decline and failure to move with the times.

EPILOGUE

The comparison of the Mohammedan Mission, on the one hand, and its applications in history, on the other, raise many critical issues that the Muslim must face honestly and boldly. Although my survey may have thrown a negative light on the manifestations of the Mission, as seen from our modern perspective, it is not permissible to generalize. What may seem negative in our view, may have been viewed positively in its own time. Thus, our task is not to pronounce judgments for or against the exegeses and solutions of the ancients, but rather to respond to the requirements of the modern consciousness without arbitrarily manipulating historical reality. Comparisons with what has gone before are necessary only because the impact of the past on the present is still very great. With or without good reason, the past is constantly quoted, appealed to, and relied on, so that a complete break with it in every case is impossible. A more appropriate approach is to evaluate it without prejudice and to refrain from considering it an ideal model and thereby impeding the Muslim's search for a firmly-founded faith and a sense of belonging free of fixations and compulsions.

I do not deny that my presentation may have dwelt on the subjective dimension of the Muslim's response to the Mission, without paying much attention to its institutional manifestations in both the distant and the more recent past, and without emphasizing the absolute commitment of many Muslims to these manifestations. Thus, I did not examine the collective dimension with all the care it deserves, and my only justification is the belief that the subjective response, on which I have focused, is usually ignored or sacrificed for the good of the nation, or rather for what is thought to be the good of the nation. I am firmly convinced that the priorities must be reversed, so that the future of this nation may be built on the free will of its members and not on established conceptions of identity or hollow outward alliances, which soon weaken and fade away when challenged and replaced by different forms of national, racial, and other alliances. Moreover, the institutionalized manifestation of the Mission, as it crystallized in the works of the scholars, is not its only manifestation in history. The Islam of the populace, or the Islam of everyday life, for instance, does not coincide with that of the scholars. As to how Islam was actually experienced by the people from one day to the next, we lack serious studies, since historians rarely took any notice of such phenomena, or only did so in order to interpret them in accordance with their own set standards.

My focus on the subjective dimension is not the consequence of an intellectual whim or an attempt to be different, but rather a product of my belief that in the same conditions all human societies are determined by the same factors and ruled by the same universal laws, regardless of any declared or hidden intentions. In the past, unity between the different elements and categories of society was guaranteed by the religions. This led to restrictions on freedom and to a stereotyping of the forms of religiousness, with penalties exacted from all those who strayed from them. However, the rise, during the past two centuries, of new factors on which social unity and solidarity may be established, and which need no religious justification, has created a real challenge for traditional religiousness. As a result of this situation, unprecedented in history, institutionalized religions were forced to give up their conventional roles under the overwhelming pressure of the new reality and thought.

The history of the two other monotheistic religions may

help us in our efforts to appreciate the present of Islam and anticipate its future. Of the main strands of Christianity, Protestantism was the first to sense the exigencies of modernity and the need to keep up with them in Western societies that witnessed the modern industrial and scientific revolution. In the same societies, Catholicism delayed changing its discourse and its practices until the 1960s, when it was obliged to adjust them in the Second Vatican Council. Christian Orthodoxy persisted in societies that had not yet reached the same level of development, that is, on which the same modernizing forces had not had an equally strong impact. Judaism, for its part is characterized by two major features. The first is its acceptance of a variety of stances due to the oppression suffered in many European societies by its adherents, who were therefore obliged to favor those elements that bound them together over those that divided them. The second feature is its association with minorities that were at some times isolated from, and at other times slowly merging into, the majorities around them. Thus, the Jews' reaction to modernity varied greatly from one group to another and from one environment to another. This feature characterized both the Jews dispersed around the world and those who settled in Palestine.

Surrounded by drastic changes, Islamic societies have not experienced a kind of modernity resulting from their own progress. Therefore, they understandably feel that the new views and values are imposed on them by a stronger party that aims at weakening Islam before destroying it, particularly as that party adheres to a different doctrine. With regard to that suspicion, Muslims in general do not differ from traditional Christians: they all look for enemies conspiring against them in the dark. The conspiracy may be an illusion, but the danger is real. There is indeed a serious threat to what they have inherited, what they have been brought up on, what they have been taught in their schools, and what they have read in their special books. They see the number of believers decreasing and the number of atheists increasing day by day. They witness the diminution of the domains in which religion used to play a major role, the open disparagement of sanctities, the drift of public and private life away from morality and religious values, and the violation, both secret and public, of these values. They watch the growing mass of confused individuals who search for the meaning of life, but fall prey to frauds and charlatans. They experience all that without any means of resisting or fighting back, and when they believe that they have discovered a way, they find themselves in the snares of terrorist groups and the whirlpool of violence and counter-violence.

There is no escape from admitting this reality, and therefore we must question its significance and its real architects, and try to ensure that all believers—Muslims and non-Muslims alike—seek the ideal way to rectify it, rather than persist in conducting futile debates in which each party displays its own views without regard to those of the others. I do not believe that there is more wickedness in the world now than there was in the past, and if our own contemporaries are living in unstable and confusing conditions, these are no more challenging, either financially or morally, than those of earlier generations. All there is to it is that phenomena change and what was formerly obscure and ascribed to fate or predestination has now been brought out into the open and solutions are sought in broad daylight for all to see.

Islamic societies are not excluded from the processes at work in other societies, even if they used to be dominated by the sole opinion of the ruler and to cover up their problems, believing that declaring them openly would be a crime against religion and society. This opacity and mystification in Islamic societies only serves those who benefit if things remain as they are, with all their flaws and drawbacks. They are the ones unaware of the poet Ahmad Shawqi's lines:

> The time of appropriation has passed, oh Pharaoh
> And the state of the tyrant has collapsed.

If Islamic societies are to participate in the creation of contemporary civilization, and not just to consume its material products, would it not be better for them if they were prepared to face the challenges that are bound to threaten the traditional Islamic system, rather than wait for a miracle that will never happen? For this to happen, two main conditions would need to be fulfilled: one would be an increase in the standard of living by modernizing the means of production, the other a joint effort of intellectuals with different opinions and different orientations.

This is not to say that certain facts and principles can be ignored or eliminated. For Muslims, modernity is of an alien origin, but its impact is universal. One of the major values it upholds, and which in fact was already embodied in the Mohammedan mission, is considering man a free and responsible *individual*, and not just a member of a group. An existence worthy of being called human must differ from that of animals, no matter how high their level of instinctual organization may be. There can be no true being by delegation but only by each individual bearing responsibility for the choices he consciously makes. To be free to think means having an intimate bond with truth, not imposed on an individual by others but attained through intuition and the dictates of an internal motivation far from any form of external pressure. However, absolute freedom contains the possibility of an amoral world, or the end of all morality, which imposes limits on freedom.

That is the role of Qur'ānic ethics, which should be considered as a line that must not be crossed. The light that guides the believer does not lack a specific history, but is, nevertheless, a light that fills the world and informs man's thought of being and the world. The believer's position in relation to the world differs from that of a scientist who measures, weighs, and analyzes. Unlike the scientist, or the philosopher, the believer listens devoutly to the words of God with his heart, regardless of all scientific, or other, certitudes. I am convinced that the drift away from Christianity as a result of liberality and individualism in Western societies will not recur at the same level in Islamic societies, because Islamic belief is centered on a text that is constantly present, and not on any one interpretation among the many provided by historical individuals. Those who regard the Islamic Mission as a call for external submission may break away from Islam, but are they true Muslims in any case? Does the message lie in formal membership of a group or in a free and deep conviction?

The Islamic sciences form a complete system, created in response to the requirements and values of ancient societies. This system must be reconstructed on new principles if it is to be fit for the conditions and values of our own age. Probably, the most important principle is to consider the Muslim, like any other individual, as possessing rights that cannot be compromised or trifled with, and that were asserted by the Universal Declaration of Human Rights and all the international conventions that confirmed them.

These rights are accompanied by certain duties, which cannot be denied either. Some duties are valid for everybody, while others apply specifically to Muslims. This reverses the traditional view of the Muslim as primarily bound by duties, with rights coming only in second place. There is less emphasis on the rights than on the obligations, and the obligations themselves are of the old discriminatory kind that favors the elite over the general public, and men over women. However, the reversal of the traditional view requires a comprehensive awareness of the modern view of the human being and new methods of education, which will break away from what has been handed down, steer clear of the obsolete, and back the future and people's legitimate aspirations to more freedom, equality, justice, and dignity.

Finally, whether or not my approach to the Mohammedan Mission and its manifestations in history is a sound one, such an attempt would encourage us to look ahead with optimism, despite the grave obstacles and challenges facing the Muslim and the backwardness impeding his progress at all levels at present. The emergence of what ᶜAbduh al-Filali-Ansāry[194] has called "a new Islamic consciousness," which we have witnessed in the past few years, suggests that the road to the future is open. All that is needed is that we take this road, casting away illusions and narrow-mindedness, and going forward with self-confidence and hard work.

[194] ᶜAbduh Filali-Ansāry, *L'islam est-il hostile à la laicité?*, Preface to the second edition, Casablanca, 1998, p. 165.

NAME INDEX

ᶜAbd al Qadir, 52
Abd al-Qāhir al-Jurgānī, 50
ᶜAbd el-Jabbar, 184
ᶜAbd el Qader, Prince, 191
ᶜAbd el-Qaher al-Baghdadi, 186
Abdel Raḥmān b. ᶜAouf, 113
ᶜAbduh al-Filali-Ansāry, 198
ᶜAbdul al-Muttalib, 28
Abdullah b. Abi Saᶜd b. al Sarḥ, 49
Abdullah b. ᶜAbbas, 125, 126
ᶜAbdullah b. Sālih, 151
Abdullah bin Jaḥsh, 38
Abdullah bin Masᶜud, 49
Abdullah bin Zayd bin Thaᶜlaba, 38
ᶜAbdullah, 26, 93
Abraham, 20, 21, 26, 42
Abu al-Hassan al-ᶜĀmiri, 150
Abū Bakr, 47, 67, 90, 101, 103–105, 111, 127, 144
Abu ᶜAbdullah, 151
Abu Dhar al Ghafārī, 113
Abu Ḥanīfa, 61, 129, 143–147, 158, 185
Abu Ḥasan al-Ashᶜari, 162
Abu Ḥassan al-ᶜAmiri, 128
Abu Ḥayān al-Tawḥīdī, 147
Abu Hurayra, 112, 125
Abu Husayn al-Basri, 168

Adam, 19, 60, 88, 107
Ahl al Kitāb, 117
Ahl as-Sunna, 190
Ahmad b. Ḥanbāl, 143-146
Ahmad Shawqi, 195
cAiād, 150
Al 'Uzaci, 185
Al Fārābī, 35, 36
Al Ḥaddād, 55
Al Jaḥiz, 105
Al Shahrastani, 35
Al-Ashcari, 186
Al-Baqlāni, 186
Al-Bukāri, 159
Al-cAbbas, 103
Al-cUzza, 29
Al-Dimashqi al-Shafici, 142
Alexander the Great, 112
Al-Ghazāli, 65, 149, 168, 186, 190
Al-Ḥallāj, 190
Al-Harmazān, 126
Al-Ḥasan, 143
cAli b. Abu Tālib, 28, 80, 172
cAli cAbdul Rāziq, 76
cAli, 103, 120, 122, 126, 144
Al-Jahm b. Safuan, 185
Al-Jaziri, 142
Al-Khattib al-Baghdadi, 81
Al-Kindī, 35, 150
Allah, 63, 68, 88, 91, 108, 149-151
cAllāl al Fāsī, 55, 168
Allāt, 29
Al-Ma'mūn (Caliph), 52, 141
Al-Majusi, 141
Al-Mansour (Caliph), 141
Al-Matrīdī, 186
Al-Mawardi, 90, 154

Al-Muᶜtasim, 52
Al-Muᶜtazilah, 148
Al-Mutawakil, 52, 125
Al-Muzni, 143
Al-Nazzām, 128, 163
Al-nuᶜman al-Ismaᶜili, 141
Al-Rāzī (Fakhreddin), 61, 168, 172, 174
Al-Sarakhsi, 116
Al-Shafiᶜi, 129, 141, 143–146, 155, 159, 160, 166
Al-Shibani, 141
Al-Tabari, 14, 47, 125, 129, 143, 146, 172, 174
Al-Tijani, 118
Al-Uzaᶜi, 116, 143, 144
Al-Wāthik, 52
Al-Zahri, 144, 176
Al-Zamakhshari, 172
Al-Zubair b. ᶜAuwām, 113
Amos, 21
Ar-Razi, 172
Ash-Shaᶜbi, 143
As-Suyuti, 34
Ataturk, Kemal, 76
At-Tusi, 172
Avicenna, 35

Baal, 19
Bani Nasr, 151
Bar'a bin Marur, 38
Bergson, Henri, 45
Buddha, 27

Caesar, Julius, 73
Castoriadis, 124
Comte, Auguste, 6
Confucius, 27
Copernicus, Nicolaus, 3

Daoud, 144
Darwin, Charles, 3
David, 89
Dumezil, Georges, 6
Durand, Gilbert, 20, 107
Durkheim, Emile, 6

Eil, 19
Eliade, Mircea, 6
Elohim, 23
Eugen Drewermann (Dr.), 92
Eve, 60, 107
Ezekiel, 21

Feuerbach, Ludwig, 6
Frazer, James, 6
Freud, Sigmund, 3

Gabriel, 32, 33, 34
Galileo, Galilei, 94
Ghaylan al-Dimashqi, 185
Gilgamesh, 19

Hazm al-Zahiri, 141
Heiler, Friedrich, 62
Hishām b. ᶜAbd el-Malek, 185
Hisham Jaᶜit, 33
Hisham Sharabi, 114

Ibn Abdel Bar, 113
Ibn Al Kalbi, 29
Ibn al-Qassim, 141
Ibn al-Riwandi, 148, 163
Ibn Bādīs, 55
Ibn ᶜAbbas, 144
Ibn ᶜAqīl, 163
Ibn Faḍlān, 90

Ibn Ḥanbāl, 158, 165, 185
Ibn Hazm al-Zahiri, 167, 168
Ibn Hazm, 35
Ibn Hishām, 14, 129
Ibn Isḥaq al-Shāṭṭibī, 168
Ibn Isḥāq, 14, 29, 129
Ibn Khaldūn, 35, 73, 90, 127, 132–136, 158, 170, 181, 182
Ibn Masᶜud, 144
Ibn Qudamah al-Ḥanbali, 141
Ibn Qutayba, 179
Ibn Rushd, 142, 149
Ibn Saᶜd, 14, 28, 129
Ibn Taymia, 35
Imam al-haramayn al-Juwaynī, 168
Isaac, 21
Ishmael, 26

Jaᶜd b. Dirham, 185
Jacob, 21
Jeremiah, 21
Jesus, 22, 27, 41, 50, 73, 89
Job, 21

Kaᶜb al-Aḥbār, 171
Khadīja, 28, 30, 32
Khaled b. ᶜAbdullah al-Qasri, 185
Khālid b. al-Walīd, 113
Khalid b. Sinān Al ᶜAbsi, 42

Le Bras, Hervé, 6
Levinas, Emmanuel, 53
Lods, 23
Lot, 21

Maḥmūd Mohammed Tāha, 56, 57, 59
Maḥmūd Sudqī (Dr.), 63
Mālik b. Nuwaira al-Tamīmī, 113

Malik, 129, 141, 143–146, 151, 158, 177
Manāh, 29
Marwān b. al-Ḥakām, 48
Marx, Karl, 6
Mohammad Abdu, 105
Mohammad al Tālibī, 47, 58
Mohammad ᶜAbed al-Jabiri, 129
Mohammad Charfi, 67
Mohammad Iqbal, 70, 87
Mohammad Taher b. ᶜAshour, 168
Mohammed b. Jarīr at-Tabari, 143, 146, 147, 172
Mohammed ᶜAbduh (Sheikh), 31, 55
Mohammed, 21, 26–30, 32–35, 37–42, 44, 50, 51, 53, 61, 62, 73–78, 80, 88, 89, 93, 101, 104, 108, 115, 120, 127, 136–138, 140, 160, 163, 164, 171, 173, 178,
Moses, 19, 27, 32, 41, 42, 50, 61, 89
MuᶜTazila, 49
Muhieddin b. ᶜArabi, 190
Munkar, 123

Nakīr, 123
Nebuchadnezzar, 50
Noah, 43

Paul, 22, 118
Pettazzoni, 6
Piaget, Jean, 114

Rashidun, 99

Saḥnoun al-Maliki, 141
Sahnun, 149
Shahab al-Din al-Sahrawardi, 190
Solomon, 76, 89
Sufiyan ath-Thawri, 115

Talḥa b. ᶜUbaid Allah, 113

^{c}Umar b. Al Khattab, 47, 75, 80, 111, 112, 118, 126, 138, 144, 151
^{c}Umar b. ^{c}Abd al ^{c}Azīz, 176
Ummayid, 99
^{c}Uthmān, 47, 48, 75, 114, 144

Wahab b. Munabih, 171
Waraqa bin Noufal, 32
Weber, Max, 37

Yahweh, 19, 20

Zayd Bin ‘Amr Bin Nufayl, 29, 144
Zoroaster, 27